Tracey Elliot-Reep

Designed and published by Tracey Elliot-Reep 2012
Photographs © Tracey Elliot-Reep
Text and sketches © Tracey Elliot-Reep
Shilstone Rocks
Widecombe-in-the-Moor
Dartmoor, Devon TQ13 7TF
England
www.traceyelliotreep.com

ISBN 978-0-9538231-8-5

CW00839920

3

GREECE

ITALY

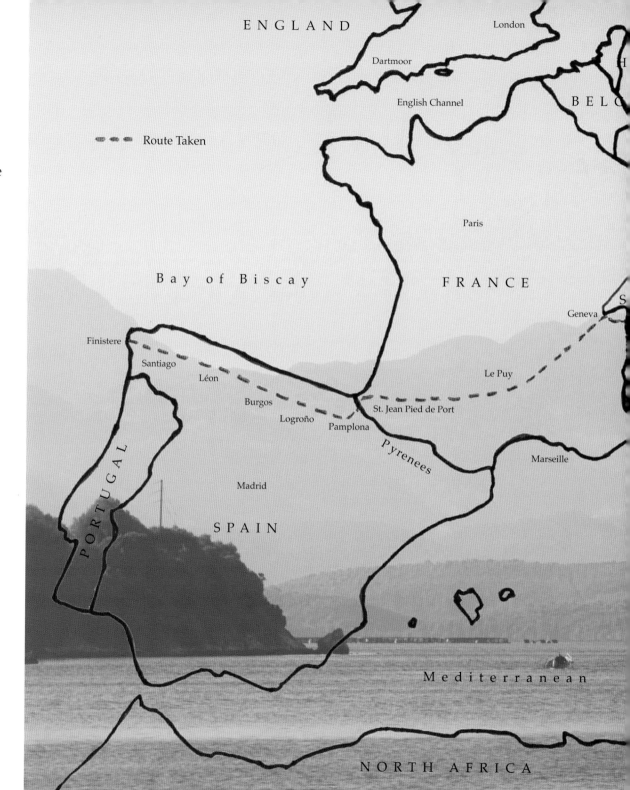

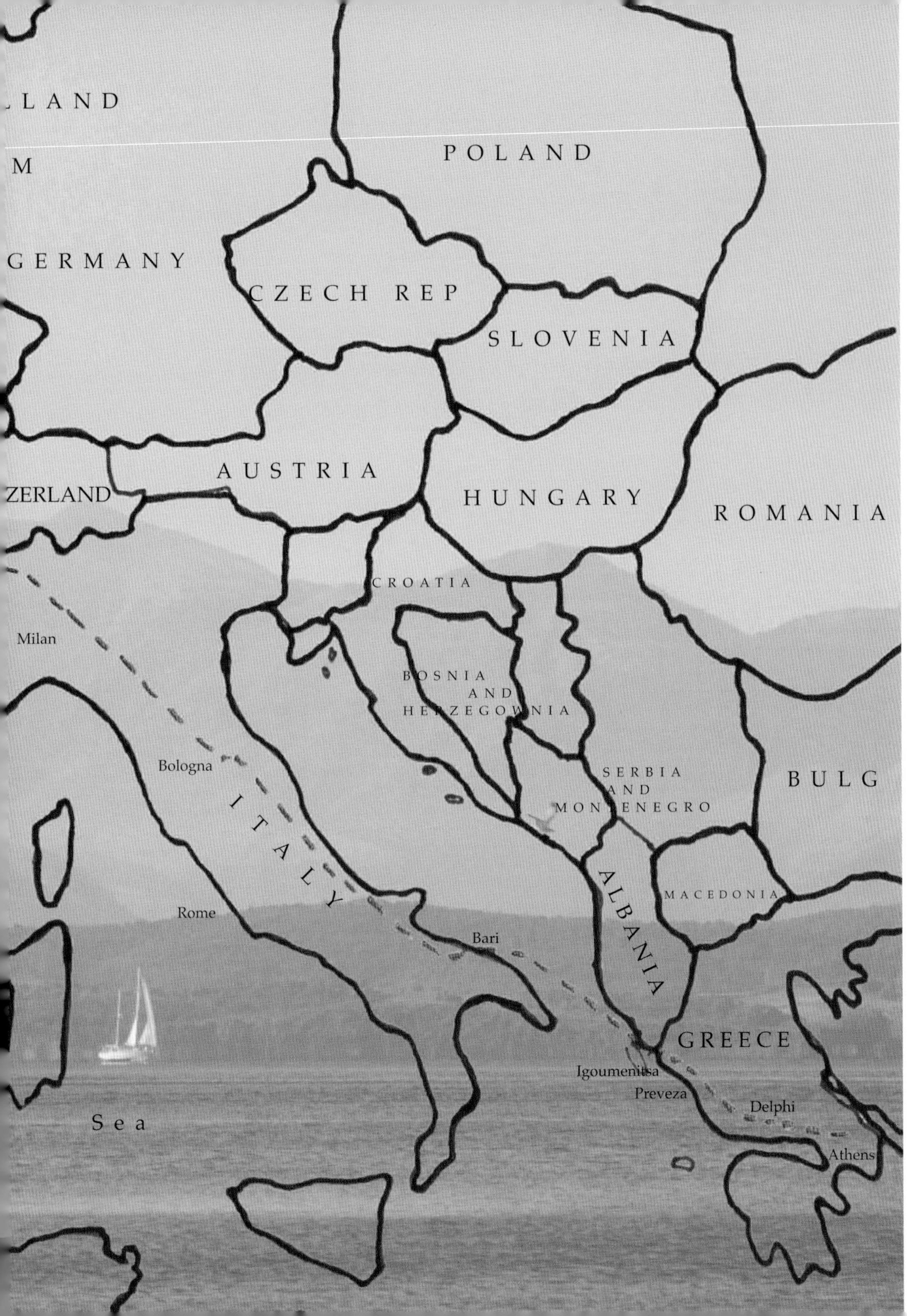

POLAND

GERMANY

CZECH REP

SLOVENIA

AUSTRIA

HUNGARY

ROMANIA

ZERLAND

CROATIA

Milan

BOSNIA
AND
HERZEGOWINA

SERBIA
AND
MONTENEGRO

BULG

Bologna

ITALY

Rome

MACEDONIA

ALBANIA

Bari

GREECE

Igoumenitsa

Preveza

Delphi

Sea

Athens

Introduction

Tracey grew up on a farm on Dartmoor, in South West England, and is still based there today, producing cards, calendars and books. After studying art and design, she worked with and sketched the animals in a circus, and taught horse riding across Europe and North America, before training as a photographer in south Wales. She worked as a freelance photojournalist for several years, when she did everything from interviewing royalty at Buckingham palace, to riding horses 2,000 miles through New Zealand to raise money for charity.

Tracey's faith in God, and her love of horses, adventure and photography, have taken her from Africa to Russia, and from Israel to Tibet. She has ridden horses from the top of Scotland to Lands End in England, around southern Ireland and Wales, and from Mexico to Canada. This, her fourth 'Riding by Faith' book, tells of another epic journey, and one of extreme contrasts – from the summer heat of Greece to the windswept pilgrim trails of northern Spain, passing through the history, culture and beauty of Italy, Switzerland and France.

1. In the beginning

Teach us to make the most of our time, so that we may grow in wisdom. Psalm 90v12 NLT

It was February, in the heart of the New Zealand summer, and I was having coffee with the lady who stocks my books in the Christchurch Cathedral bookshop. As I strolled back to my car, I thought: "This must be one of the most tranquil and beautiful cities in the world."

That night, I stayed with a customer on the coast at Akaroa, and the next day I left much later than intended to return to Christchurch to make another book delivery. As I reached the outskirts, it felt as if my car had suffered a tyre blow-out – abruptly swerving backwards and forwards across the road. I pulled over, but was surprised to find that none of them were punctured. And then I felt the ground shaking. The next six hours were spent stuck in gridlocked traffic, on swaying bridges, amid mud and water which poured from broken pipes after a catastrophic earthquake.

Your time is limited so don't waste it living someone else's life -Steve Jobs Co-founder of Apple

Only later did I discover that buildings in the street I had been heading for had collapsed, crushing cars and people. I had narrowly escaped – it reminded me how fragile and brief life can be.

I left New Zealand and on my way home to Dartmoor, in south west England, I stopped off in Colorado to give some talks on my horse riding adventures. Here, I met a lady from Nebraska who suggested I got in touch with Lord Bates – a British politician who serves in the House of Lords, and who was soon to begin a 'peace walk' all the way from Greece to London. Once I got home, I contacted Lord Bates, and agreed to take photographs of him on some sections of his walk. I just took it for granted that I'd travel with horses – I didn't intend to walk all the way!

I asked God that if this was His guiding, I'd need a reliable contact in Greece, as I could only imagine what kind of horses disreputable dealers might try to sell me.

Three weeks before I left for Greece, I visited the Channel Islands to give a fundraising presentation on behalf of the Riding for the Disabled charity. Here, I met a Greek lady called Helly who put me in touch with her cousin, Costas, a racehorse breeder in Athens. He kindly agreed to help me out, so I described what I wanted: light-coloured ponies, about 14.2 hands (147.3 cms), very quiet in traffic, but forward movers. Costas related this to a horse dealer, called Kiriakos, whose wife spoke some English.

For we walk by faith, not by sight. - 2 Corinthians 5v7 NKJ

"You would like a black horse? What sex? A girl or boy?" she asked.

"Mare or gelding, boy but not man horse," I told her, trying to explain that I didn't want a stallion.

She called back later: "We have found a nice one but it is thin."

"No, I can't start with a thin horse, they only lose weight," I replied, concerned that "thin" could mean emaciated (although at least I'd be rescuing the poor animal!). "Can I look before I buy?"

"No," came the answer. "And we need €1,000 up front."

"Don't do it," said the Irish voice from Western Union when I tried to wire them the money. "I tell you it's a scam."

"Oh God, this is tough," I said. Before my previous rides, I've always seen my horses first, to be sure they were right for me. But then a verse came to my mind: 'We walk by faith not by sight'.

This wasn't the only challenge. "You're not serious. How will you manage the language?" a friend asked. I'd been dyslexic and struggled with English, let alone foreign languages!

My mother, used to my previous expeditions, but still concerned, took me to Exeter station and we staggered to the train, carrying saddles, bridles and equipment. Fortunately a friend, Jackie, met me at Guildford. She and her husband Pete bought me a better mobile phone and Jackie took me shopping to buy another long-sleeved shirt for my journey, while the eldest of their seven children looked up useful Greek words on the internet.

"God, this would be crazy if I weren't sure this was Your idea!" I breathed, as they helped me onto the coach to Heathrow airport. I settled down to learn my first Greek words: kalispera (good evening), kalimara (good morning), efaristo (thank you), parakalo (please), alogo (horse), trofi alogon (horse food) and posos (how much).

GREECE – HELLAS

2. Athens

"You will find that Costas can never say no," said Annita Valvis as she and her husband Costas greeted me at the airport. But then came the bad news: "Customs want €90 to deliver your pack saddle to our house and €450 in duties."

"But that is more than the old pack saddle I used crossing the USA is worth!"

"This is Greece," Costas replied, nonchalantly – obviously used to bureaucracy. They took me to get a local sim card for my phone and then out to supper, where we talked about our lives over a delicious Greek meal.

"I was a horseman from five years old," he told me. "I started with a donkey, when we lived in the Sudan, and rode it to school." The family went on to train racehorses, winning the Sudan Derby three times, and were second three times in the Greek Derby. Today, they also train horses in France.

"Now, they're saying they won't let the pack go until you give them the consignment number and pay the duty," Annita stated at breakfast the following morning, after having a loud argument over the phone.

I called my friend Greg in America, who had sent it over. It was the middle of the night in Texas, but he didn't seem to mind. The number he gave me for the package didn't satisfy customs, so I had to wake him up a second time.

Costas kindly took me to the customs office, who were still asking for more than the old pack saddle was worth. After we'd seen seven different officials, he said: "You need to have a lot of arguments here before they understand. It takes patience." But after we'd toured the buildings, talking and arguing, he added: "We'll have to return on Monday – maybe then they will let us have the saddle!"

Costas took me to their farm, one hour north of Athens, and offered to take me back the following Monday. But by then, we found the price had gone up by another €100 Euros, just for storing it over the weekend!

Then Costas and Annita arrived with the pack saddle having managed to get it out of customs at a much lower price. "That's Greek bureaucracy," he shrugged, "we explained and we argued!"

3. Greek horses

"He's asking about his money again!" Costa chuckled as he put the phone down. "Today we will see if you like your horses or not. The moment of truth!"

I was feeling both apprehensive and excited as we drove off. With Greece on the verge of bankruptcy, the horse dealer desperately needed money, and conversations with his wife hadn't given me confidence. Everything hinged on the divinely orchestrated contact with Costas, who was respected by the dealer.

On the way, we passed several petrol stations with empty forecourts, until Costas stopped at one with a long queue. I asked why he'd chosen such a busy one. "I only refuel at two garages in Athens," he explained. "The others mix the fuel with other liquids and my car doesn't run well."

"160 million olive trees in Greece. They're a gift of God as they don't need a lot of care," he informed me as we sped through miles of dry, hilly land, dotted with silver green trees.

I sighed to myself: "Going to Greece, buying unseen ponies and riding them back to England? God, if this wasn't Your idea this would be crazy!" And I took another deep breath as we walked down the long row of empty racehorse stables. A solidly-built horse dealer slid a stall gate open and my heart sank as a small, 13.3 hand, dark bay gelding showed us the whites of his eyes and nervously swung his hindquarters towards us.

"He's nine," Costas translated, but the brand new passport told me he was 12 and he appeared older still. His name was Ermis and he had a pretty face, with a star, although his head was too large for his short neck. A heavily matted, dull coat covered a prominent backbone, beneath which hung a bloated stomach – probably the result of never having been wormed. My mind flashed back to the original offer of a 'thin pony' – if this wasn't the thin one, then the other must be emaciated!

I asked the dealer where his ponies came from. "All over Greece," came the blunt reply. I could only imagine that this gelding had lived his life on the end of a rope probably on rough ground where he couldn't roll – how else could his coat have become so matted?

The dealer pushed another door open to reveal a pretty, five-year-old, dark grey mare called Yoana, who had obviously had much kinder treatment... although as she raised her muzzle to my face enquiringly, I noticed her lower eyelid had been ripped and hung down her cheek.

"What breed are they?" I enquired.

"Greek horses," replied the dealer, avoiding eye contact.

I looked at the passports and asked where the tetanus and flu injections were recorded.

"The vet said it wasn't necessary," Costas translated, which surprised me – all horses travelling overseas needed injections. The dealer clearly wanted to get as much money out of me as possible. I knew these horses were overpriced – much more than I'd have considered paying if I'd seen them first. But I had to walk by faith, not by sight. This journey was going to need ponies who were not just good looking, but also bomb proof and tough.

I asked Costas to make sure the dealer signed a receipt to confirm he'd received cash for the ponies, passports and shoeing. I'd actually brought my own receipts, anticipating that the dealer wouldn't have any paperwork of his own.

"The shoes look good – and with the studs you asked for!" Costas commented, studying their hooves.

"God, may their shoes wear well and stay on for however long it takes us to travel through Greece," I asked, knowing there weren't many horses here and it would be difficult to get shoes replaced.

Although I felt the ponies were overpriced, Costas and Annita made up for this with their kind help, and invited me to stay at their farm for several days, while I prepared and exercised the ponies and fuelled them up with plenty of oats. They generously gave me fresh organic vegetables, goat milk, meat and olives.

To avoid the heat, I took the ponies out to exercise early in the morning and late in the evening. On the first occasion, they had a kicking match, and I held my breath that neither of them would be hurt. Eventually, Ermis established himself as the leader over Yoana, who was very mare-ish in her behaviour and less than half his age.

I wormed and bathed them both in the warm sun. Yoana wiggled her top lip with delight as I massaged her coat with the curry comb, producing soapy suds, but Ermis nervously shuffled and swung his hind quarters towards the hose. I could only assume that he'd never been brushed before in his life, let alone bathed, as his matted coat came out in clumps. A prominent white scar across his nose was a telling sign – evidence that his halter had been too tight.

Yoana was more laid back but occasionally stubborn. She didn't like to follow Ermis so I tried tying her to the back of Ermis' saddle. This was a mistake, as she stopped and pulled the saddle D straight out of the back of the saddle – not a good start. Now I only had attachments left on either side, so I had to lead her and have my arm stretched instead.

Months later, a friend told me that in Greek legend, Ermis (or Hermes) was the messenger, who was "fleet of foot", and patron of boundaries and the travellers who cross them. What's more, the Hebrew origin for Yoana (or Ioanna) is "God has favoured me". They had picked good names for the journey!

Let the peace of God act as empire deciding and settling all things that arise in your heart, and be thankful. Colossians 1v15 AMP

"Eggs are a good food for the brain," said Costas handing me a bagful. "They should keep for three days, but no longer in this heat." He also gave me tins of sardines, nuts and nut bars mixed with honey, adding: "Alexander the Great fed his army on these before he went into battle!" Annita handed me a complete map of Greece – all I had were pages ripped out of a book of European road maps.

"Greece is not like when I was young," Costas warned. "Beware of the immigrants. Better to be suspicious and keep your distance. Don't tell them you are from England – they will know you must have money – and be sure no one sees where you camp. These are hard and dangerous times in Greece. If you get through Albania you will be okay."

"How can I tell who to trust?" I asked, feeling rather desperate. "I can only speak a few words of Greek."

"You will know by their faces," he said, pointing people out as we passed through a town. "See those two men? They are from Albania. And those are gypsies. Be careful."

I was feeling rather overwhelmed and would have to be led by God's peace or lack of it in my heart. After all the warnings, I didn't really feel like going anywhere, especially launching out across Greece and leaving the security of the farm. With all its wildlife, it was like a nature reserve for me and the ponies. In the cool of the evening, I would sit out in front of the house and listen to the frogs croaking in the water channels, sounding like ducks, and the tiny hooting owls sitting in the trees opposite.

14

4. Launching out across Greece

Fear and faith are present with us every day. You choose which one will rule your life. - Bob Gass

I couldn't stay. I had to launch myself across Greece before it got any hotter and try to catch up with Lord Bates, who was already far to the north. So I left early, my pack overflowing with as many oats as I could fit in. This, combined with the intense heat, meant we never got beyond a slow walk. Somehow, I needed to lighten the load and always start at daybreak – as soon as it was bright enough for us to be seen on the roads.

First, I aimed to reach Diana's house – a friend of my godmother's who lived near Preveza on the west coast – and from there I would go north to Albania and meet up with Lord Bates. Costas had suggested that I use farm tracks to avoid the roads, but they often came to a dead end and I'd have to double back. On one track, an irate man sped towards me in his van, shaking his fist, and skidded to a halt in a cloud of dust. I couldn't tell if he was Greek or Romanian, only that he was very angry. To avoid further incidents, I returned to the main road, but here farmers roared along the hard shoulder in their tractors, waving at me to move over.

At a garage, I used my limited Greek to ask if my ponies could have some water, but the attendant ignored me. Another man, reeking of alcohol, came to my rescue, but after watering my ponies he wanted me to go back to his place. So I rode on, until I heard someone shouting. I turned around, relieved to see a young girl who invited us for a drink.

I couldn't find any shade from the midday sun, just a grassy track to graze the ponies. After several hours in the open I felt baked by the sun, and headed for another garage hoping to find more water. "Look!" yelled the attendant, storming out in a rage and pointing behind me at my ponies' droppings. I apologised and cleared them into the verge, which was littered with rubbish. When I asked for water, a man stepped out of a smart car, signalling for money with his thumb and fingers.

The ponies were so thirsty that I hadn't even filled the bucket before they plunged their heads in, splashing water over me and the forecourt. Japanese tourists frantically photographed the chaos, which probably saved me from any more of the attendant's wrath.

There is more to life than increasing its speed - Gandhi

I soon discovered that in Greece, many people drove like maniacs, with little regard for road signs, rules or speed limits. They blasted their horns at me and I really wasn't sure if they were being friendly or telling me to get off the road. Whatever the reason, it gave me a headache. I stuck religiously to the verge all the way, but when I saw a curving bridge with no hard shoulder and only two lanes separated by double yellow lines, I anxiously looked for an alternative. Randomly, I took a track off to the right which headed down to railway lines, hoping to find a safer route. I didn't know which was more dangerous – crossing the bridge or four sets of rails – so once I got there, I tied the ponies up and considered my options. Praying, I encouraged the ponies to cross the tracks quickly, although they didn't understand the hurry.

Later that day, after slogging along more busy roads, a car pulled over in front of us and a young man came over to say hello. After so much noise and stress I was relieved to meet someone friendly. He introduced himself as Dennis and said he used to have thoroughbred horses, but the Greek economy was so bad that he was off to find work in Australia. As he walked back to his car, he suddenly swivelled around and returned to us. "You can come and stay with my family," he said. "We have a spare room, 15 minutes up the road."

I dismounted and led Ermis, as we travelled faster this way, but after an hour of walking I was overheating, the pain in my head had increased and I was feeling sick. I found a shady spot under a tree beside the road and sat there until my body cooled down. Being Greek, the ponies didn't seem bothered by the heat, and grazed contentedly until I remounted and we moved on. I wondered if Dennis might have regretted his impulsive invitation, but then I spotted him waiting for us.

"It was longer than 15 minutes wasn't it!" he said, apologetically, as he guided us up a quiet mountainside road to his family home. Once we were there, he helped me unpack and feed the ponies, who were grazing in the garden. My head was splitting and my eyes were red, so after supper I went straight to sleep – waking only to drink my way through several litres of water.

Drink, drink and drink again, and get into the shade at midday. I was learning my lesson. The following day I found a small tree to hide me from the sun and moved as its shadow shifted. As it was a secluded spot, I put on my shorts and took off my shirt, desperate to let the breeze cool my body. However my rest was interrupted by biting ants and caterpillars dropping on me from the branches. The ponies weren't much better off – I could see them frantically kicking at vicious biting flies. We all desperately needed fly spray.

After five hours of fighting the insects and trying to keep cool, I
packed up the ponies. As we rode off, a strong wind snatched my
hat. I watched it roll on its brim down the centre of the main road,
but managed to grab it before it got squashed by a passing vehicle.
The evening light was better for photographs and this, combined
with a cool breeze and much less traffic, made me feel that perhaps
riding across Greece was not so bad after all.

But my period of calm was interrupted when a transit van
stopped and two men greeted me, speaking broken English with an
American accent. Costas' warnings were fresh in my mind – I was
in a remote spot, with a camera in my hand, and I knew this wasn't
a good situation to be in. Feeling rather rude, I ignored them,
quickly remounted and tried to persuade the reluctant ponies to
trot.

I was looking out for a good camp spot when I passed a large
restaurant with a group of people sitting outside. They called out
and beckoned for me to come over. I was cautious to begin with, but
they appeared genuinely friendly. They offered me water for the
ponies and suggested I make camp on the mountain slope opposite
the restaurant. Once I had unpacked, fed and tethered the ponies
out to grass, I returned to eat lamb chops and laugh with the Greeks
as we all struggled to converse in our two languages. Later, I
rejoined the ponies and relaxed on my bed roll on the mountain side
– grateful for the altitude, the coolness and the lack of flying insects
in the magnificent, moonlit starry sky. I awoke early the next day
and was packed up by the time one of the men from the restaurant,
Thermis, shouted up the mountain: "Greek coffee!"

With sweat running down my face, I felt like a kettle on the boil as I led the ponies up to Arachova town, its houses clinging to the side of a mountain. Amazingly, four lanes of traffic were somehow squeezed into almost one, constricted by the buildings and parked vehicles on either side of the road. At first, I rode, thinking this would be safer because drivers would see us, but I caused a traffic jam as large tourist coaches backed up behind us. Then Ermis, with a deep disliking for drains, refused to walk over one, so I had to quickly dismount and lead him past before anyone lost their temper.

Once out of the confines of the town, the road widened, allowing room for the traffic to pass us. We continued on our way to Delphi, and arrived to find it packed with coaches and people. We cooled down in a little alcove, in the shade of some trees, but it wasn't long before a crowd of tourists joined us with their packed lunches, so we had to move back into the heat.

Arachova

I spotted a pipe gushing water beside the road, so I just had to stop to fill up my red bucket. A man was shouting at me from across the road as the traffic skirted by, and adept bus drivers swung their coaches around a nearby corner, missing us by inches. I was thankful for quiet ponies. As soon as the man across the road discovered I was English, he gave me a thumbs up – I was relieved that the English must be considered to be okay in Greece!

Delphi was clearly a tourist destination, and has been for centuries. Pilgrims once came from all over Europe to consult the oracle at the sanctuary of Apollo. In the early sixth century it became a Christian site and is still visited by hordes of tourists today – so many, in fact, that there was nowhere to secure the ponies so I could take a quick look. The closest I was going to get was the site map at the main entrance, so I had to settle for seeing its great pillars from a distance.

5. Delphi

"Bravo!" someone shouted. I was relieved that Delphi people were so friendly, even when we blocked a one way street. An elderly couple offered me a fruit drink and a shop attendant gave me a big bottle of water and the ponies some apples, which they loved – I had to stop Yoana entering the shop, looking for more delicious treats. An Italian bus driver gave me two more small bottles of water, which I immediately drank, and invited me to cool off in his air-conditioned bus. I'd have loved to, but I motioned to my ponies, suggesting that they'd have to join me, and we laughed.

On the outskirts of Delphi I found a secluded, shady spot with grass for the ponies. I settled down to eat and opened a plastic bag, only to quickly shut it again, as the smell from the last of Costas' eggs made my stomach churn.

I was relaxing, writing my diary, when a stallion appeared. He tried to climb the fence to get to my ponies, and managed to get his front legs over the wire. I quickly moved the ponies and then struggled to untangle him under the hot sun. I returned to my shady spot as quickly as I could, seeking out the best spot to catch the breeze, but by five o'clock, with only three hours of daylight left, I knew I had to make a move. I'd noticed that this far south, the light faded much earlier than it does in England.

The stallion was still racing up and down the fence, so I couldn't bring the ponies back to their saddlery and load up in the shade. Instead, I had to make several journeys, dragging the packs to them through the blazing sunshine, which made the packing up even more exhausting than usual. Using both hands, I tested the bags to make sure the weight was evenly distributed before loading them into the panniers on the pack saddle. Lastly, I added the light bedroll and roped it all securely together.

As I was harnessing Yoana, and flicking her tail out from the breeching, she kicked out at me, catching the inside of my right knee. Fortunately, I was standing close to her – if I'd been any further away, she could have broken my leg. Immediately, I reprimanded her (she never attempted to kick me again), but my knee was already swelling up. It was painful to mount and to sit in the saddle. However, I had no choice but to ride, to avoid overheating.

21

Being on the road was stressful, with fast traffic, tight bends and often no hard shoulder. I had to concentrate to keep the ponies at the very edge of the road, but without sliding into the sloping drain. That evening, Ermis slipped over into the ditch and I rolled off, just as a car was passing. We were both shaken, and I added a few more bruises to my collection. It was at times like this, as we were crossing Greece, that I wondered what I was doing. I was lame, worn out by the intense heat, never-ending traffic and lack of water, and being continually attacked by savage, biting flies.

A German lady kindly stopped and asked me if I needed anything. She gave me a lukewarm bottle of water and held the ponies as I repeatedly launched a bucket, on the end of a rope, into a fast-flowing water channel. I kept going until the ponies had had their fill.

"Don't continue in the dark here, will you," she warned. "This is not a safe area." She told me she'd lived here for eight years, and gave me her phone number. Her friendliness gave me the boost I needed to press on and find somewhere to pitch my tent before it got dark.

I was keen to camp on the high ground, before we descended towards the sea and into even greater heat. I found an old olive grove that looked deserted. Here, I tethered the ponies and erected my tent – for insect rather than rain protection – but it was like a sauna inside, only adding to my discomfort. My bruised leg was so painful that I needed both hands to lift it on top of my sleeping bag.

That night, I slipped in and out of sleep – the result of an aching leg and the neighbourhood dogs who never seemed to draw breath. I was up before light, not even pausing for my all-important cup of tea, and hurried to pack up before the sun rose and the temperature soared. I thought back several years, to a time when I'd camped at over 10,000 feet in the North American Rockies, at the same time of year. It was hard to believe that I would wake up to frost on my tent and look forward to the sun appearing over the mountains to warm me up!

I took a smaller road, winding through a coastal plain called the Sea of Olives, containing more than 400,000 trees. But then I arrived at a junction, where there was no alternative but to join the traffic-laden main road, which was edged with a ditch running straight into the city of Itea. I rode, as it made us more noticeable, but while Ermis took no notice of the dangerous trucks skimming by, he continually shied at the white line and ditch along the edge of the road. I quickly decided it was safer to lead them.

"Oh God, it's too hot and I hate being on these roads," I cried, choking back the tears. But every time I thought of giving up, I also thought of my two little Greek ponies, who I simply couldn't leave behind.

On the outskirts of Itea, I found a pavement wide enough for the ponies and had composed myself by the time we reached a garage and a water tap. I was relieved to find an owner who could speak English and showed him my map, asking how to get off the main road.

"There is no other way," he said, pointing to my map. "You have to follow this narrow road, busy with trucks, until you pass this quarry. It is dangerous, but here you can get onto this small mountain road. It's very steep, zig-zagging," he added, demonstrating the slope with his arm. "It will take you much longer to get to where you are heading."

Camp spot in old olive grove.

6. Mountain views

Can God prepare a table in the wilderness? Psalm 78v19 NKJ

I had no other choice but stick to the verge, pray, and move as quickly as possible… which was never very quick with my Greek ponies. One driver overtook us and just as he was driving towards a blind bend, he turned and took a photo. No wonder, I thought, there are so many memorial shrines beside the roads.

At last we reached the mountain road and left the coastal highway. It was steep, but I didn't mind, as the higher we ascended into the mountain breezes, the less stressed I felt. I did wonder where I'd find water and grass in this arid wilderness, but then thanked God, knowing that He would somehow provide for us. Up and up we went, along the steep, zig-zagging road. We were only overtaken by small, struggling, top heavy pick-ups, spilling over with hay and furniture, straining with their weight, whose drivers looked at us curiously.

In the village of Tritaia, I was so thankful to find a tap in a little alcove, where I watered the ponies and washed their saddle towels. I tethered the ponies out in a rough spot of long grass by the church, while I sheltered in the shade against its big white wall. With water, time to wait for the temperature to cool, and no particular destination for that day, I made myself several cups of tea. It made up for missing my early morning cup, in my dash to beat the heat.

As I wrote my diary, I thought of some simple things I hadn't fully appreciated, which I now considered luxuries: a cup of tea, a shower and feeling cool! As I wrote and pondered, I had to continually move to remain in the shade, as the scorching sun rounded the wall. By four o'clock my shady refuge was dazzling white, signalling that it was time to leave.

"Mulas!" said a large, friendly man, comparing my ponies and their packs to mules. "This one is like the horses the army took into Albania in the war," he said, pointing to Ermis. He asked me where I was going.

"Preveza, on the west coast," I replied, and he directed me to a left turn, a little way back down the mountain. He also invited me back to his place for a shower – it was tempting, but I decided to keep going and to retrace our steps out of the village.

Itea city on the coastal plain where there was an ancient racecourse and where the allies in 1917 based themselves as a supply route which ran to the eastern front.

Twenty years from now you will be more disappointed by the things you didn't do than by the ones you did do. So throw off the bowlines, sail away from the safe harbor. Catch the tradewinds in your sails. Explore. Dream. Discover. – Mark Twain

I had no idea where we'd camp that night. I couldn't even read or pronounce the Greek place names on the signposts, which only occasionally matched those on my loose-leaf roadmap. Before leaving home, I'd ordered a European atlas, but it weighed five kilos and was much too heavy to carry, so using a scalpel I'd carefully cut out the maps of the countries I was intending to travel through, including Greece, Albania, Serbia, Croatia, Italy and France.

I appreciated those few hours when it was comfortable to be on the move – early in the morning and after six in the evening. This was especially true high up in the mountains, away from the stressful roads, where we couldn't afford to put a foot wrong and be hit by a vehicle. Here, we could enjoy the evening light, and just had to trust that we'd be directed to a good place to camp.

The view leaving the village of Tritaia back across to Arachova and beneath Delphi town.

7. Agia Efthymia

You chart the path ahead of me and tell me where to stop and rest. Psalm 139v3 NLT

As I rode through Agia Efthymia, I spotted a little girl with long dark hair watching me through binoculars over a garden wall.

"Ya!" I called out to her, but she ran away, so I continued up the road to a covered drainpipe, stretching the width of the road. Ermis stubbornly refused to step over it, and as we struggled I heard a lady calling.

"Coffee?" she asked, using hand signals to show me what she meant. I'm not a coffee drinker – especially the strong, Greek variety – but I was attracted by her friendly greeting, so I dismounted and led Ermis back to a gate in the wall where the little girl had been hiding. After giving me a choice of cool drinks, a man and an older woman appeared. I pointed to myself and said my name, and the man wrote theirs on a piece of paper. He was called Andreas, Foteini was his wife and their daughter (with the binoculars!) was Anastasia. I was reluctant to leave as they were such friendly people, but it was after seven and I knew that I had less than an hour of light left to find a safe place to camp. I looked over their wall, pointed at some scrubland, then to the ponies, and then put my hands together against my head, miming sleep. They seemed pleased with the idea. After we'd watered the ponies, I pointed to Anastasia and then to Ermis, and her father lifted her into the saddle. With a big smile, she rode Ermis around the back of the house to our overnight camp spot.

It was so good to have a shower and put my shorts on, although the bruising had spread up and down from my knee. Fortunately, it now looked worse than it felt.

As we drank refreshments on the veranda, visitors came and went including Spiros and his wife Voula, who taught English in Athens. "Oh God - Perfect timing!" I exclaimed. "A Greek lady who teaches English arrives in the same place, at the same time!"

The bells make music!

"You certainly came to the right house – Andreas is the mayor!" Voula told me, "Spiras, my husband was before him." She acted as interpreter as Andreas and his family took me up Mount Gionas, the highest mountain in southern Greece to show me the distant clustered lights of Delphi, Arahova, and Galaxidi on the coast. At 10pm, when I was ready for bed, they took me to an attractive restaurant, where we were joined by Spiros and Voulas' three children. The Greek food was delicious, with olives, fresh and colourful vegetables and platefuls of lamb.

"Young ba- ba," said Andreas, pointing to a plate of lamb chops. "Old ba-ba," he added, pointing to another! After the meal, at about midnight, the dancing started. Everyone had their own style – and I could see the influence of the Turkish belly dancers, from a time when the Turkish Ottoman Empire occupied Greece for five hundred years.

We were up at 6.30 the following morning, and Andreas drove us up Mount Gionas when the light was good, where I enjoyed filming and photographing the cows, knee deep in water, cooling themselves in large ponds. "In early May, this area is a mass of beautiful wild flowers," said Voula, translating for Andreas, and I regretted not being there earlier on my ride. Due to the heat, only a few limp plants survived.

"Greek honey is the best. The bees collect the pollen from the pines and wild flowers," she informed me, as we passed a row of colourful hives. I could smell the wild thyme, sage and camomile, which the locals collected and dried for their teas.

My trail of discovery continued down the mountain to a local vineyard, where we tasted some wine. From here, we went to look at some wild pigs, and then on to meet a shepherd and his small flock on the outskirts of the village.

"The sound of the bells is musical," he told me, with Voula's help. "Each bell is different. In the past they were all handmade, but that tradition is now dying out. The bells not only tell me where the animals are but they make music."

29

Galaxide

8. Greek Orthodox

I felt as if I'd stepped back into ancient Biblical times. Halfway up a mountain, on a twisting gravel road, stood a statuesque, bearded, Greek Orthodox priest, dressed in flowing black robes and holding a tall stick. He was gazing out over the village of Agia Efthymia and the great expanse beyond, to the sea.

Foteini spoke to him and he gave her a pretty beaded necklace holding a crucifix, to give to me, along with permission to photograph and film during the Pentecost service. I felt honoured to have this opportunity, as it was such an interesting and colourful event.

As the readings hummed out through loud speakers, people continually arrived and climbed the steps to the church porch, where they lit a candle and placed it carefully alongside many others in a box-shaped alcove. After bowing, they kissed the saint's image, framed with a white and pink wreath, before proceeding into the little church, already tightly packed with mostly older, sun-wrinkled faces. The walls were lined with rows of framed portraits, depicting saints, set uniformly against the same rich, gold background. Every so often the congregation would spill out of the church and follow the priest in a procession around the building, and on one occasion out of the gate, before returning inside. Those who couldn't fit into the church gathered in the porch and chatted to people who came and went throughout the long service.

Papas Dimitris

"When we get to the church, we buy a candle at a very low price –
50c or one Euro," Voula explained. "The moment of the candle
lighting is sacred, and this is depicted in the faces of the faithful. It is
when we usually think of a small prayer or make a promise to God."
She continued: "In every Orthodox church there is a picture of Mary
and Jesus together with the honoured saint. In this one, the main
icon represents the Holy Trinity in whose honour the church was
built in 1995. After the candle lighting, the faithful kiss the Saint's
toes as a token of worship and respect. The women are much more
expressive than the men in church, and kiss more pictures."

"Why do they circuit the church? What will they do next?" I asked Voula, trying to anticipate the priests' next move – they'd caught me by surprise when they first began to swing the incense and suddenly paraded around the building.

"The procession around the church is a ritual on important days," Voula told me. "The priest carries the holy icon, while the Bible is carried by a member of the church board. Incense is burned, and the congregation bow their heads and make the sign of the cross."

I had been fortunate to witness the ritual of the bread blessing – a special event which commemorates the time when Jesus blessed the loaves and fish in the desert. Nowadays these breads tend to be flavoured with anise seeds and are offered by members of the congregation – usually the women – as an act of piety. The bread is blessed and after the Mass it is divided among the faithful. While I was filming, one of the 'Papas' offered me some with a smile, and I gratefully accepted, but unfortunately my mind was on the filming, and I left it behind, along with a whole bagful of bread that someone else had given me. I thought about this longingly once I was back on my ride.

I'm not sure what the older people felt about me filming, but as the priest had given me permission they accepted me, and the usher was most helpful in ensuring I had a clear view. At the end I was touched when a young boy gave me an intricate, gold-painted, little card depicting Mary and Jesus with halos, which I put straight in my pocket.

"Why do they chant the readings through a loudspeaker?" I asked Voula.

"The mass amplification outside the church happens on special days," she explained. "It's so that the word of God reaches every house of the community."

9. Lake Mornou

The eyes are the window of the soul. - proverb

Foteini pointed to her eye, then my eye, placed her hand on her heart and said, "be careful", just as she had on the day we met. I gulped back the tears as I rode away, thinking of these people who had been so good to me, and carrying their gift: a heavy pot of mountain honey.

In many villages, I saw memorials to those who died in World War II. Agia Efthymia is listed as one of the 'Towns and Villages of Martyrdom'. The Axis forces shot 37 people here and more than 80 others died when the town was bombed and burnt. Its people have a proud history of courage in adversity – the Greeks made 11 attempts for independence and one of their leaders, the Bishop of Salona, was born in the town. He made an alliance with the Venetian army and navy in an attempt to overcome Ottoman domination, but was killed in battle.

Slowly, we continued westwards through the barren mountains, always on the lookout for a well-hidden camping spot with good grass and trees. I knew there were snakes, but so far I had only seen squashed ones on the road. I counted seven that day alone!

I was happy to find a secluded spot, but just as I was settling down for the night, a man appeared with two big dogs. My heart sank, thinking we'd been discovered, but decided to make the most of this encounter by giving him a friendly wave. I showed him with my map, using sign language to indicate where I was going. "Problem!" he said, pointing to the steep mountain road that I'd intended to follow, and directing me northwards past a reservoir.

The next day, while my ponies grazed and I sheltered from the midday heat, I suddenly heard my name. I thought I'd imagined it, but then Andreas' smiling face appeared, and he handed me a packet of biscuits! As neither of us could speak the other's language, he handed me his phone, and I spoke to Voula. She told me that Andreas was out on a job for the electricity board and wanted to check I was okay.

The following morning, while I was still circumnavigating the reservoir, and trying to get the ponies down to the water for a drink, he hailed me again. He scrambled down the slope, giving us the thumbs up, to ask if we were okay. I gave the thumbs up back, adding "nay efaristo" (yes thanks), followed by "nero" (water), and pointed to the reservoir and then the ponies. "Siga, siga!" (slowly, slowly!) he laughed, indicating walking with his fingers, and waved as he left.

I slid down to the reservoir, filled up my red bucket and climbed back to the ponies, only to find they didn't want to drink! I was beginning to see that they preferred a big drink at midday or early afternoon. Ermis took small sips, while Yoana would gulp the whole bucket down in one go!

A departing photo with my new friends in Agia Efthymia.

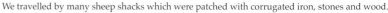
We travelled by many sheep shacks which were patched with corrugated iron, stones and wood.

The cloud cover and the cool breeze were a welcome relief, but the wind became so strong that I had to tie my hat tightly under my chin and bend my head as we forged onwards. Thunder and lightning followed, but I didn't put on my waterproofs as I liked the coolness of the rain. Despite this, the flies continued to irritate the ponies - especially Yoana, who kept throwing her head around, jerking the lead rope and my arm. I'd tried, without success, to buy fly spray for horses, but don't think the locals had ever heard of it. So our movement consisted of one or two steps forwards, a jerk on the arm, and then a pause as one of both ponies used a hind leg to flick the biting flies off their stomachs.

It was much more peaceful on the mountain roads, but still I had to keep alert for vehicles speeding around the twisting corners. I hoped the drivers would be more cautious here, as there were cattle on the roads. I met a friendly old woman with her cows and we tried to have a conversation, but couldn't understand each other.

After leaving Lake Nasos and leading the ponies down a narrow, zigzagging lane, littered with fallen rocks, I arrived at an inn – the first settlement I'd seen for hours.

"Don't eat my flowers!" said a slim, dark girl, translating for the elderly patron. "And be careful of the snakes," she added as I tethered the ponies out in some rare long grass. Most verges were cropped short by hungry cows and sheep.

"We are the only people here, so why don't you join us?" added the girl, who introduced herself as a singer called Mary, and to her friend Nikos, a lawyer from Patra. They both spoke fluent English, which was such a relief, as I knew I'd missed so much by being unable to speak Greek.

The inn was more a taxidermist's museum than a restaurant. On the walls hung photos of dead wild pigs, and the counters were crowded with all forms of stuffed creatures – from the tiniest bird to large wild cats. The patron was glued to a large, loud TV screen in the corner of the room, almost oblivious to anything else, even when a large man and my new friends started discussing ways for me to bypass the main roads to Preveza. The man pointed a big finger at my map. "You can't avoid Nafpaktos – a big city on the coast," he said, with Mary's help.

As they left, Mary and Nikos gave me their phone numbers. "You know that in Greece you have two friends. Just call us," she said, adding: "Your smile will get you anywhere!"

> "Hence we will not say that Greeks fight like heroes, but that heroes fight like Greeks."
> – Winston Churchill

I'd set off early to make the most of the cool morning, as usual, when an open-topped truck, loaded with barrels and a big chestnut horse, pulled up in front of us, and out jumped a man I'd met in the restaurant the previous night. He mimed loading my ponies onto his truck, wrote €300 on a piece of paper, said "Preveza", and mimed drink and sleep.

"Efaristo ahi (no thanks)," I replied, but he was so persistent that I became concerned he'd return. There was no way to avoid him on this quiet country road, so I called Annita Valis in Athens and asked her to explain I didn't want a lift. In fact, I did see him again – this time his truck was full, although he still insisted on giving me his phone number - even though we couldn't speak the same language!

I led the ponies 30 kilometres down the winding roads, and right into the busy city of Nafpaktos. We walked a further 10 kilometres through crowded streets, as vehicles skimmed by, until I spied a garage hose pipe and I asked a man in blue overalls if I could use it. He turned out to be a teacher, and told me all about Greek history – from the Spartans through to Greek resistance during World War II. I learnt how British Commonwealth troops fought alongside the Greeks, were vastly outnumbered and out-gunned, and how the British managed to evacuate 50,000 troops. We talked for several hours, as the ponies grazed, until I realised it was seven o'clock and I needed to find a safe place to camp outside the town. As I left, his parting gift was Winston Churchill's quote, "hence we will not say that Greeks fight like heroes, but that heroes fight like Greeks", which gave me a much better understanding of their temperament and their manic driving. This was soon confirmed when some boys on loud motorbikes tried to intimidate me by repeatedly drawing up alongside, revving their engines and screaming away, making even my bomb-proof ponies jump.

At the edge of the town I saw some hoof prints on the side of the road and heard a whinny.

"Where are you going?" asked a man in a white shirt and jeans, standing at a gate leading to a dressage ménage and stables.

"Preveza," I replied, and he slid back the gates to invite us in. We followed him to his stables, where he helped me unpack and introduced himself as George. My ponies were delighted to be given some sweet meal grain, as we'd finished all our oats. He then showed me his vacant house, gave me a key and said I could stay the night.

"I have to go now, but if you want something to eat I can come back at ten."

"Thanks so much but I will be asleep by nine," I replied, as I was so tired after our long, stressful walk. "Thank you so much – it's just so wonderful to have a secure place to spend the night."

I awoke at 6.30, and met George as I made my way back to the corral.

"We didn't get to know each other," he remarked when I said I had to leave, and thanked him for his kindness. His large Friesian horse also whinnied a goodbye.

I wished I'd stayed longer, but I was conscious that Diana, my contact in Preveza on the west coast, would soon be going away. Having experienced the dangerous Greek highways, lined with memorials, and knowing that Lord Bates was walking on main roads through Europe, it had become ever more obvious that this wasn't the way to travel with ponies. I realised I needed to catch a ferry to Italy instead, and I knew I'd need Diana's help with the Greek paperwork.

Lake Mornou

10. Kapsorrachi - hitch hiking mouse

Be helpful. when you see a person without a smile, give him yours.
- Zig Ziglar

Above: We passed many roadside shrines.
Below: Hospitality at a Zeygaraki cafe.

"I should have asked George where to buy fly spray," I said, as we jerked along, stopping and starting as the ponies battled with the insects. Poor Yoana had bites all over her neck.

I'd swapped the packsaddle onto Ermis, who had a bigger head but a smaller body than Yoana, which meant all the straps had to be tightened. My soles were so sore from walking on hot roads that I rode Yoana, but she wasn't used to going in front and shied frequently, draining my energy and made me hotter. Ermis also had the habit of stopping suddenly whenever he did a dropping, yanking the rope. With cars speeding by, I couldn't risk letting go, so the rope bruised my stomach and shredded my gloves.

During one particularly heavy thunderstorm I sheltered under an overhanging roof beside a huge, vicious Rottweiler, who barked loudly and flung himself against his cage – I hoped it wouldn't break. I then took the winding mountain roads to Kapsorrachi and Lake Trichonida, on whose beautiful shores I found a secluded camp spot… amongst rubbish, broken furniture, plastic bottles and human waste. I was continually surprised by the amount of litter strewn across Greece, even in beauty spots.

"Well, you must have good balance!" I exclaimed, as a mouse leapt out from under the wooden cross bars, supporting the saddle bags.

We were spotted by a local shepherd, who was soon followed by an official-looking man in a long-sleeved shirt. I greeted him with a friendly "kali spera!", but this time my smile didn't melt his grim expression. I indicated that I was heading for Preveza, while trying hard not to laugh at Yoana who was comically itching her bottom to remove flies. He said absolutely nothing and just walked away, making me feel uncomfortable. I sensed that I was in an unfriendly environment, which made me uneasy, but there wasn't enough light to continue, so I calmed myself by reading Psalm 91 out loud.

As I packed up, early the following morning, the same mouse popped out of my saddlebag and scampered up the big tree to which the ponies were tied. He stopped and looked down at us.

"You can come if you like," I told him, but he declined and continued up the tree, so we left him in his new environment.

The roads were narrow and the cars fast. Mounted on Ermis, I had to concentrate to stop him from shying away from the drains and into the traffic. As I passed a restaurant in Zevgaraki, a lady signalled to me to stop for a drink. The manager, Dimitris, who owned horses, washed the ponies' legs and then provided them with an armful of hay. They then cooked me fried eggs, served with a fresh salad sprinkled with feta, and offered me the luxury of a shower, which I gratefully accepted, washing away several days of sweat and grime.

Camp at Kapsorrachi on the banks of Lake Trichonida

11. Hiding in the olive groves

He who dwells in the secret place of the Most High.
Shall abide under the shadow of the Almighty. Psalm 91 NKJ

"The Greeks have a knack of being able to squeeze through crowded streets, but they drive too fast. That's why there are so many crashes," said Dimitris, proprietor of the restaurant, through my latest interpreter.

In Greece, there were just two types of road: high-speed highways or winding mountain roads. I had to continue along a busy main road until I found a smaller road heading for Lisimachia – which was confirmed by a man who leapt out of his car to give me a bottles of juice and water. We continued through a thunderstorm, past olive groves, looking out for somewhere to camp. A man on a quad bike rode past me several times but no one saw us as we disappeared into the trees. Then I heard shouting and although I didn't understand the words, I knew people were out looking for us. I moved beyond the trees and into some scrubland, praying that the ponies wouldn't make a noise. The men seemed determined to find us, and I heard a motorbike racing up and down, getting ever closer to our hiding place.

"God, don't let them see us," I whispered, willing it to get dark quickly. I knew we'd be safe to camp here, but not if they forced us back on the road. My stomach churned as the motorbike grew louder… and I sighed with relief as the rider turned away, obviously not seeing the hoof prints in the damp earth. "Thank you God for hiding us," I breathed, as it roared away.

At four in the morning, I had a cup of tea and then packed up in the dark, using my head torch. I intended to leave the area before anyone saw us, hoping to cover some miles before the midday heat. We joined a major trunk road and I thanked God for the protection of His angels, as there were so many trucks and cars rushing by.

We were passing a café when some people beckoned me over for a drink. I asked for water for the ponies and tethered them in the shade, before accepting a drink myself. I was cooling off under the canopy of broad leaves when the proprietor offered me some lamb, stored in a cage to protect it from the flies. Holding a big cleaver, he asked me which piece I would like. There seemed to be just a trace of meat attached to one inch of solid fat, so I chose the smallest part I could see, not wanting to offend. "Don't you like it?" he asked, when I'd eaten as much cold lamb's fat as I could manage.

I couldn't face going anywhere until the heat subsided, and it seemed that the people in the café were doing much the same thing. I concluded that some Greeks drove like maniacs to coffee bars and then sat there all day.

"Are you wealthy?" asked the proprietor, translated by a schoolboy, which took me by surprise. It got me thinking about our different cultures. Although I didn't own any property, I did have nine horses, which I couldn't part with as we'd shared adventures in different parts of the world. I also had a business which I'd started 19 years ago, selling just six postcards, living in a caravan with my dog. With little money, but faith and plenty of hard work, it had grown to the point where I could head off on adventures. I still had to rough it, but I did have the freedom to travel. So yes, I was wealthy, but in a more meaningful way.

Do not trust in the uncertainty of riches but in God who gives us richly all things to enjoy.
1 Timothy 6v17 NKJ

42

Katouna

Everyone seemed to have an opinion about the best route to Preveza. "You can go all night if you stick to the main road" was one crazy suggestion from someone who clearly knew very little about horses or the dangerous traffic. But I thanked them as I left, and soon found a smaller side road, which was much longer but more peaceful.

Some guards at an army barracks kindly gave me a bottle of water as I passed by, leading the ponies and looking for a place to camp. Both sides of the road were fenced, so I marched on as the sun sank lower. Eventually, I spied a break in the fence. When I could hear no approaching traffic, I quickly led the ponies through the gap, down an embankment and into another old olive grove.

There wasn't much grazing, and the ground was too hard for my tent pegs, so I had to rely on stones to stop me slipping down the slope, but I was thankful to have found a safe, quiet place with a stunning view over a lake.

Entering Katouna the next morning, I watered the ponies at a garage, even though it was closed, and met a friendly blonde lady who pointed out the route through the town. I passed groups of women dressed in black, and many other people out walking or sitting in coffee bars, so I guessed it must be Sunday. Men beckoned to me to join them, but I kept going until I reached a square, where I spotted the woman who had given me directions earlier. She introduced herself as Irini, and with the help of a teenaged translator, I learnt that she was a doctor, originally from Albania.

"Aren't you frightened?" she asked.

"I trust in God," I replied. I really wished I could to talk to her, sensing that it must take a strong woman to be a female doctor in Greece. However, I appreciated her presence and encouragement as she bought me coffee, water, a ham roll and a rose, whose petals quickly wilted in the heat.

Irini in the Katouna square.

12. Vonítsa

Yoana was a good doer - always eating!

I led the ponies to keep them right at the edge of the road, but I was sweating, overheated and tense as the traffic skimmed past us. So I was glad when a sturdy Greek man motioned me over for a drink to sit under a cool canopy of broad leaves with him and his wife. Our conversation was non-existent as I sipped very strong black coffee accompanied by sugared peaches – a local delicacy. When I couldn't delay getting back on the road any longer, he kindly gave me four home-grown cucumbers.

Later that evening, as I turned off down a narrow lane, a car screeched to a halt, only just avoiding us. The driver scowled at me with a look that said: "how dare you be on the road". It reminded me of something I'd heard: that European funding had allowed brand new roads to be built, but too quickly, and the rapid change from donkeys to fast cars had caused many deaths.

I dropped down a bank into a rough field and hid the ponies behind some trees, avoiding a snake and some large spiders' webs. I heard a car stop and I held my breath, thinking our hideout had been spotted… but then flying through the air came a bag of rubbish and landed nearby!

"Why don't they just use the bins?!" I exclaimed. "They treat their beautiful country like a rubbish dump!" Everywhere I looked, on the sides of the roads or tumbling down mountainsides, there were hundreds of plastic bottles, old plastic chairs, tables and mattresses – products that would never biodegrade. Sometimes the stench of rotting animal carcasses, dumped beside the road, was so bad that my stomach churned and I had to hold my breath as I passed.

"Italy has got to be easier to travel through, please God?" I whispered.

The beautiful Venetian causeway at Vonitsa.

At six the following morning we left our hiding place and rejoined the main road. I wondered why they bothered with road signs, because no one seemed to take any notice – drivers still felt compelled to overtake, even in fast-moving traffic. So not only did I have to listen out for vehicles approaching from behind, but I also had to look out for others bearing down on us on the wrong side of the road. Every time I saw a zig-zag sign, indicating sharp bends, my heart filled with dread – especially when hemmed in by railings and competing with the trucks for limited road space.

We reached Vonitsa – an old Venetian town defended by a 17th century fortress, with a beautiful, decorative causeway stretching out into the harbour. At the time of the Ottoman Empire the Venetians occupied Corfu and much of the coast. I'd heard that the Greek people much preferred living under Venetian rule as they were Christians, and didn't spit-roast the priests as the Ottomans apparently did!

In the town I asked for oats. "This is Greece!" shrugged one man, while another directed me, through a combination of Greek and hand signals, to a store outside the town. Despite my basic grasp of Greek directions, I wondered if I really was on the right road, so I was relieved to find a grain silo, where I was offered a 40kg sack of oats. To reduce the weight, and much to the ponies' delight, I immediately poured some on the ground for them to eat on the spot. I then divided the remainder into two sacks, which I loaded onto Yoana, which doubled the weight she carried. As we continued on our way, I saw that the extra weight was causing the saddle panniers to rip. Feeling hot and bothered, I tied the ponies in some shade while I unloaded the oats. I was wondering what to do when I spotted a man in his garden. Using my own mixture of Greek words and sign language, I asked him if I could leave the oats there and said I'd come back to collect it.

We headed for the tunnel under the estuary, connecting the peninsula with Preveza, and met up with Diana and her friend Margaret (who looked so English with her dog on a lead!). It was fabulous to hear that Diana had arranged with the authorities for the ponies to be transported through the tunnel. The Greek efficiency took me by surprise, as I'd only given Diana an estimated time of arrival, but within minutes a trailer had arrived. The next pleasant surprise was that I was charged nothing – not even the expensive toll. At the other end, Diana introduced me to Theodosis, the manager for Teos A-Aktusa, so I thanked him and his company for allowing me to travel through the tunnel for free.

Diana leading Ermis along the quay in Preveza.

Diana with Ermis in her garden in Agios Thomas.

"The vet didn't have fly spray for horses, but I've got you some spray for dogs!" said Diana. This was the best possible gift – it brought relief to us all and without the distractions the ponies picked up speed.

On the other side of the tunnel, Diana escorted us through Preveza and down to the quayside, amid moored yachts and plush hotels. I hoped the ponies wouldn't leave any droppings! My prayer was answered, and we made it through without mishap.

She then directed me to her home in Agios Thomas, about eight kilometres up the coast. The little house stood right on the edge of the sea, only separated from the water by a small road and a mass of high bamboo. The ponies were delighted to discover plums in her garden, so I had to tether them so they couldn't do any more damage to the prized trees. After everything they'd been through, these plums were exceptionally tasty!

"I hope the ponies didn't damage your trees," I said apologetically.

"They needed pruning… it's just in a different way to do it," Diana responded casually.

It was fun to shower in a little outside enclosure, but the water in the hosepipe became so hot from the midday sun that it had to be poured into a bucket to cool off. My ponies also enjoyed themselves, eating the oats which Margaret's friends had collected from where I'd left them. For breakfast, I ate delicious, ripe oranges, picked from her garden.

Diana first came to Greece in 1964 as a young widow, and worked as a nurse. "I gave immunisation jabs," she said. "I showed young girls how to do it, but had to teach them to wash their hands and boil the needles first." Diana told me many stories of her life in the mountains. "It really was a great adventure. I was widowed at such an early age that I didn't know what to do – it saved my life. When I first bought this house it didn't have piped water or electricity, and I was the first person in the village to have a lavatory!

"The mountain villages were very primitive – I've seen a lot of change since I arrived. Back then you'd see old women with great loads on their backs. They'd walk five miles up the mountain to collect water."

Diana also introduced me to all her cats. "The neighbours like them too – they'd rather have cats on their patio, than rats, mice and snakes!"

I'd really enjoyed hearing her stories and having a rest, but I needed to make arrangements to go to Italy.

"We're not a farm you know," came the sarcastic reply from a representative of the ferry company. We caused further confusion when we visited the Ministry vet in Preveza – they clearly hadn't dealt with anything like this before.

"We will contact Athens," a woman told us. "There are many problems. Come back tomorrow morning." So the following day we returned to the Ministry vet, only to be greeted with: "It is not possible to transport your horses to Italy!"

13. Preveza – official papers

Consider it pure joy, whenever you face trials of many kinds,
because you know that the testing of your faith developes perserverance. James 1v2 NIV

"But with my God all things are possible!" I said, as I'd already made a firm decision: even when the dangerous traffic, flies and heat exhaustion were getting too much for me, and I was close to giving up, I knew that I could never leave my ponies in Greece. However, neither the Ministry in Preveza nor in Athens seemed to know what to do about it.

"They should have had their tetanus and flu injections in Athens," the Ministry vet told me.

"I did pay for them to be done," I replied, and called the horse dealer who'd told me they weren't needed. I handed my phone over.

"He doesn't know," she said, handing it back, adding: "I want to try and help you but I've never come across this before. My previous job was inspecting fruit imported from Africa! Come back tomorrow."

Since I arrived we'd been to the Ministry every morning – even Diana, who was used to Greek ways, was getting tired of all the bureaucracy. Trying to be practical, I arranged for my laptop and a few other bits and pieces to be sent home to lighten the load. The first courier I spoke to recommended I used their competitor across the street because they were cheaper!

"If they like you, they will bend over backwards to help," Diana remarked.

On our way back, the taxi driver was talking about the bad economic situation in Greece.

"I have to pay tax, but many don't," he said, adding that tens of thousands of Greek professionals had emigrated to America.

"The English and Greeks have a very special relationship," Diana informed me as we sat in the cool of her porch. "Lord Byron is revered here – he was the first person to alert the western world to the plight of the Greeks, who had been under Ottoman rule for 500 years. Then Churchill, himself a Greek scholar, negotiated with Stalin to prevent this country coming under Russian control, even though he had to give up some other territories in the process."

Ermis and Yoana weren't quite sure about the sea and the salty water, but they enjoyed their holiday in Diana's beach house garden!

"He's expensive," warned Annita from Athens as she gave me the number for a horse transporter, who confirmed that the ponies needed both tetanus and flu jabs. However, the good news was that he did have space to carry them from Igoumentsa to Italy on July 5, and he also had a horse contact in Italy, which was necessary in order for the Ministry to issue export papers. So I had one week to complete the paperwork and ride to the port, further to the north.

"I have never really dealt with horses before, but I will try to help you," said Dimitris, Margaret's local vet, coming to our rescue. He was Greek, but had worked in Germany and also spoke fluent English. "There is big bureaucracy with this!"

After speaking to the Ministry vets and the horse transporter, he shrugged: "I will order the tetanus and flu from Athens now. This is Greece. Patience, patience!"

"The first word you learn in Greece is 'permeate' (wait)!" added Margaret, but I didn't have much time. After the injections, the ponies would need to remain calm for three days, or their immunity systems could be weakened. We'd already been with Diana for six days, had run out of oats and eaten her grass, so I asked Dimitris where I could buy more oats or hay. In the meantime, I found patches of grass around the village, including the church grounds.

The following evening Dimitris arrived with a couple of bales of hay and the flu and tetanus injections.

"This is all they have in Greece!" he said, injecting a dog's microchip into their necks. "Now let's hope they will give you the papers before the country goes on strike, so you can get to the port on time." He added: "I just charge you for the chip and injections but not my time."

"You are great!" I replied, really touched by his generosity and effort.

"You will need more papers, ten days after you arrive in Italy," explained the Ministry vet.

"Like a criminal on parole, you will have to report to the police every ten days!" commented Dimitris.

On the eve of a national strike, another Ministry vet arrived by motorbike to check the ponies. On tenterhooks, I returned the next day to collect the papers and with Dimitris' help, we managed to get them signed just before the country ground to a standstill.

"Tell me it's okay now," Dimitris said, in a concerned voice.

"Yes, thanks God and thanks to you and all my friends here!" I laughed. "Now we must catch the ferry!"

A tortoise eating the petals in Diana's garden.

"Who's that lightweight on my back?" asked Ermis as Dimitris the vet led his son onto the beach.

St.Thomas harbour in the Ambracian Gulf.

The fishing harbour at St. Thomas with Preveza in the background. Preveza was built by Pyrrhus, King of Eprios around 1200 AD and guards the entrance to the Ambracian Gulf where the famous

14. The Ambracian Gulf

The small fishing boats left early every morning and trickled back into the harbour after 7am, spending several hours sorting through their nets. The prawns were so big! Diana and I enjoyed eating at the fish restaurant at the waterside, just where the boats were tied up.

battle of Actium took place in 31BC when the future emperor Augustus routed the fleet of his rival Antony, who was accompanied by Cleopatra, Queen of Egypt.

The Ambracian Gulf is one of the most significant wetland habitats in Greece, with extensive reed beds and a huge range of birds, including one of the very few remaining colonies of silver pelicans in Europe. However, I heard some bad news from a fisherman, who spoke some English: "In ten years there will be no more fishing, as the water in the gulf has been polluted by 64 intensive fish farms. They use highly concentrated food which poisons the water for other fish and organisms." He added: "The farmers now use much more water, so there is less flowing into the gulf to wash the pollution out to sea."

15. Nikopolis

Nikopolis, meaning 'victory city', was founded in 31BC to celebrate the victory of Octavian over Antony and Cleopatra, who were trying to safeguard Egypt's independence from Rome.

Geographically, it was well positioned between Rome and Greece, with harbours on the Ionian Sea and Ambracious Coast. Nikopolis was considered the third most significant city of the Roman Empire, and boasted a theatre seating 22,000 people. Many inhabitants of the surrounding area were forced to settle here after their cities were destroyed. It was walled, first by the Romans and later by the Byzantines.

The city began to decline after the earthquake of 373, and raids by the Goths and Vandals, and was abandoned in the 11th century. As I rode through, I saw several well preserved mosaic floors, and parts of the impressive Byzantine ramparts still stood strong and tall, towering above us.

16. Overdressed on the coast!

Despite resting at St.Thomas for nine days and being eight kilos lighter, Ermis and Yoana were still not keen to leave, or even trot, and when we arrived at the beach they stubbornly refused to move at all. To avoid the main coastal road, I dragged them through the sand, which was so tiring – like trudging through deep snow.

Thankfully there was a breeze on the coast, but I still needed to protect myself from the sun. I wore a long-sleeved shirt, sunglasses, factor 30 face cream, gloves, jodhpurs and half chaps (even though I seemed to be walking more than riding). I felt very overdressed when I rounded one headland and stumbled on sunbathers wearing nothing at all!

Further up the beach I came upon a resort which vibrated with music – a very different side to the Greece that I had experienced so far. Row upon row of sun loungers were shaded by large umbrellas, but they had only two occupants. I gave them a wave, and they invited us over for a drink, introducing themselves as Greek father and son, now living in Germany. I asked why they were the only people on the beach.

"All these loungers would usually be filled with tourists. Greece is in a very bad shape," they told me. We chatted a little, I thanked them for our drinks and waved goodbye.

Further up the beach I passed a tall, young African, from Senegal, who was selling bracelets. His eyes were bloodshot and his teeth were black and rotten. "Times are tough, would you like to buy a good luck bracelet?" he asked.

"No thank you, I trust in God, not luck," I replied, and pressed on through the deep sand. I was soon dodging volleyballs as I entered another massive and much more populated beach resort, with throbbing music and bodies packed tightly together on rows of sun loungers. I stayed the night nearby here, and was so tired I didn't get packed up until 9am the next day, by which time it was already too hot. I followed the coast road past more sunbathers, packed in like sardines.

A blonde lady called us over for a drink, invited us to stay for breakfast and gave me a bag of bread and jam, which I squashed into my saddlebag. It was noon by the time I left the resort, slipping past a group of Africans, planning the day's sales strategy. I led the ponies up a steep, zig-zagging road, sweat pouring off my face and down my back, stopping wherever I could find some shade.

At a village at the top, called Loutsa, a group of children were enthralled by Ermis, (after being kicked by Yoana, I kept her away from them). I was grateful when they escorted me to the correct turning, practising their English, as it would have been difficult for me to find. Just one vehicle passed me on this quiet, winding lane, sprinkled with sheep droppings.

As I was leading the ponies down the mountain, and through a village at siesta time, a black and white, pointer-type dog joined us. He seemed to like our company and whenever we stopped – usually where there was grass – he stopped too. When I asked a glamorous lady driver for directions (which consisted of saying a place name and pointing), and she sent us in the opposite direction, our new companion came too.

A short distance along this curving road the same lady invited us into her garden. The dog tried to follow us in and was chased away, but he found a place where he could see us, sat down and waited. The hospitable lady invited me to sit in the shade of the pergola, and with the help of a teenaged neighbour acting as translator, generously served me up a plateful of spaghetti and chicken. After several hours I repacked the ponies.

"When you come again, just shout Maria!" she said. I thanked her, waved goodbye and set off with the dog alongside us, as if he'd been there all along. But then we reached the kind of main road I always dreaded: without a verge and with cars speeding by at speeds approaching 90mph.

"You can't come with us anymore," I told the dog. "I'm sorry, but this road is too dangerous for you." Of course he took no notice, and stood there in the middle of the road, while impatient drivers blasted their horns, looking at me with his beautiful eyes.

"I tell you – you can't come with us," I shouted, shooing him away, worried that he'd get run over. I'd have loved his company, and he could have shared my food, but I was booked on a ferry in a few days time. It had taken nine days to get the ponies' papers in order – what would it take to get the paperwork for a stray dog? We'd end up missing the ferry, and I didn't know if I'd find another horse transporter. I continued to wrestle with my thoughts, trying to work out how I could get him to Italy, then France and then home to England.

Yoana and Ermis couldn't work out what was happening as I led them back into the safety of a quieter road, picked up a stone and threw it so that it landed near the dog – perhaps as many others had done in the past. I absolutely hated doing this, but I didn't want him to be killed on the road. He looked at me with puzzlement in those beautiful eyes, before walking off with his tail between his legs. As he made his way up the opposite slope, he looked back at us. I turned the ponies away, with tears running down my face, and couldn't bear to look back. There were so many stray dogs in Greece, like the dirty little dishevelled dog that I'd passed on the pavement several times in Preveza – just sitting there as if to say: "can't someone take me home and love me?" Margaret's little dog had been found abandoned on the beach, but had been one of the fortunate ones to find a good home.

17. Hoofsteps at dawn

*By His mercies we have been kept from complete destruction.
Great is His faithfulness.
His mercies begin afresh each day. Lam 3v22 NLT*

Ten kilometres up the road I spied an open expanse of long, dried grass, and an inviting opening in the fence. I quickly urged Ermis and Yoana through the gap and hid them behind some trees. I then trampled down some grass to make room for my tent, and moved a gang of large, orange and black striped spiders, who were eye-balling me.

When my alarm went off, at 5.30am the next day, I thought I heard the sound of hooves on tarmac. Suddenly all my senses were alert – I wasn't imagining it, and I could also hear trucks slowing down. I pulled on my boots and noticed that Ermis wasn't where he'd been tethered the previous night. I ran through the long grass, scrambled over the fence and saw him walking along the main road. In my haste, I tripped and bashed my knee on the tarmac, startling Ermis who began to trot. I limped towards him, caught him and led him back into the grass. I could see that the bowline knot under his chin had come loose, so I vowed in future to tie two knots, at both ends of the rope, to prevent it from happening again. I was so grateful as I later heard of a horse being killed on a main road and causing a serious accident.

We passed the turning to Parga – a very beautiful town on the coast, which I'd intended to ride through, but I didn't want to share the narrow road with numerous tour buses which were heading in that direction.

"Thank you God for your angels, keeping us safe," I'd often say, as we travelled along these roads, and I'd try to find things to be thankful for, like brief moments of shade, or the relative cool of the mornings and evenings.

At Kosina, I took refuge under a big tree beside a church, unloaded the ponies and tethered them to graze among the litter. I found a tap in the church courtyard to rinse their saddle towels and then lay down on my bedroll. As we left, an ambulance man was clearly worried to see me leading the ponies in 35 degrees of heat, and motioned for me to get on Ermis to save me from the shimmering black tarmac. It did feel as if we were riding over an open oven, and sweat ran down my face, neck and back, as though I was in a sauna. But it was now 5pm so I was optimistic that it would soon get cooler.

"Fresca!" shouted a tall man, cooking on a stove behind an Italian truck, and pointing to his frying pan, full of spaghetti and fresh vegetables. Struggling to remember Italian for 'yes', I tried 'si', to which he nodded and handed me a plate piled high with food. I was grateful for a good meal and learnt my next word of Italian: "grazie" (thank you). Through sign language I worked out that he'd been driving back and forth, carrying fish from Preveza to Brindisi, for 12 years.

I continued on my way and a little while later the big Italian in his big truck beeped as he passed us. It cheered me up, and reminded me that I was going to Italy! Then, just as we were getting into that nice time of the evening with the temperature cooled and the shadows grew long, a car drew up alongside us.

"I am a vet. Can I do anything for you? Do you need anything, at no charge?" asked a man in dark glasses, introducing himself as Panos, short for Panagiotis.

"I'm okay thank you," I replied, "but I'd really love to get some horse food."

He told me to call him when I got to my destination that night – a field belonging to a friend of Diana's, called Patrick.

"Panos you are a definite Godsend!" I told him when he brought the much-appreciated hay.

"Do you know Christ?" Panos asked abruptly, taking me by surprise.

"Yes, I do know Jesus Christ!" I confirmed. "I asked Him into my heart to be my Lord and saviour when I was 19."

"I hadn't intended to come along this road, but my clients had called me three times insisting that I come. I have been praying to meet another Christian," he added.

I stayed in a room in Plataria for a few nights. In the mornings and evenings, Diana's friend, Patrick, gave me a lift so that I could feed and water the ponies, and it was he who told me about the accident involving a horse which had got onto the road. A truck had seen it and slowed down, but a vehicle behind the truck had overtaken it, killed the horse, and overturned. The dead animal was left in Patrick's gateway for days in the heat. The incident with Ermis was still fresh in my mind, and I was so thankful that God and His angels were looking out for us.

Panos was so helpful and told me what I needed to get rid of the horrid, arrow-like flies which crawled under Yoana's and Ermis' tails and clung to the soft skin beneath. Yoana was always trying to kick them away but they clung like limpets, and even when I flicked them off they immediately crawled back. Ermis must have lived all his life with this constant irritation, and had a mass of them under his tail until Panos smeared on some special ointment. He also gave me some veterinary supplies to take with me. "There is no charge," he told me.

One evening, Panos showed me the road that I'd need to travel along to the port at Igoumenitsa. My heart was heavy, as I'd come to loathe these twisting, narrow main roads between the cliffs and the sea. There was no hard shoulder, and not enough room for the large trucks, travelling to the port, to pass us if vehicles were coming in the opposite direction.

"God, I can't travel on this road. Maybe I should ask the horse transporter to come and collect me so I can avoid the last 15km?," I pleaded.

"You have got safely though Greece on these dangerous roads. I know – I am Greek!" said Panos. "But this road is especially dangerous and we want to get you safely to the port." He told me he had a friend who would take us, and I was so thankful… although I was worried when his friend picked us up and then drove us in the opposite direction. I phoned Panos, who told me it was only because he wanted to avoid the police who were doing vehicle checks.

I was so relieved to get there that I didn't mind tethering my ponies under some trees and waiting from 11 in the morning to almost 11 at night.

I couldn't find any water at the port, so Panos bought bottled water for the ponies to drink while we waited.

18. Greek farewell

But the just shall stay alive by his faith. - Habakkuk 2v4 NKJ

The police passed by several times, and stopped to ask questions.

"Aren't you afraid?" one of them asked.

"I trust in God for my protection," I told him.

"Sure – we all do," he replied sarcastically. "But two weeks ago the place was packed with illegal immigrants from Africa. Your horses could have been eaten, and I don't know what would have happened to you."

"Well, I'm just glad that God got me here tonight, not two weeks ago!" I said. It was hard to explain the difference between religion, and having a real, living relationship with God through Jesus – listening, trusting and being directed by God through one's life.

"You know they eat horses in Italy?" he continued.

"Well, they will not be eating mine," I replied firmly.

There were lots of police vehicles milling around the port and I could imagine it was a hotspot for all sorts of illegal happenings. But my main concern was missing the ferry, as the horse transporter still hadn't arrived.

To unpathed waters, undreamed shores. - William Shakepearc

"I tell you these are not ponies, okay?" Panos told me sternly, when he came to say goodbye. "These are Greek horses, descended from the ones used by Alexander the Great to build his Greek empire!" He continued, "not everyone would consider Alexander to be a good man, and both Napoleon and Hitler considered him to be their inspiration."

Literally at the eleventh hour, the transporter turned up. There followed a frantic rush to load the packs and the ponies into this very luxurious truck. My little Greek horses had their own stalls, looking small and insignificant beside big, expensive competition horses!

Thanks to God's protection, we'd made it across Greece. I'd seen a very different side of the country to the one that most tourists glimpse from their air-conditioned buses. We'd slowly clip-clopped along winding mountain roads and fast, dangerous highways, in the heat, accompanied by flies. And we'd met people who were real gems, and who really made all the difference to the journey. As we left Igoumenitsa after midnight, I smiled at Panos' serious words of farewell: "You are now leaving Greece, but be careful. Rome is the next empire – Okay?!"

19. Arrival in Bologna

We should make plans - counting on God to direct us. Proverbs 16v9 TLB

As the huge truck disembarked onto Italian soil at Bari, I was expecting an investigation of the horses' papers and passports, but no one was there, so we continued inland. I was taught some basic Italian words by the drivers, Mike and Kiriakos, and by Alex who was travelling with her horse from a dressage competition in Turkey to another in Western Europe. I later found that they weren't altogether correct – I should have known better than to learn Italian words from Greeks!

I had thought we'd get out at Ancona, so I could travel through Tuscany but they had no stable contact in the area, so I continued with them to the destination marked on the official papers, Club Cavalli, on the outskirts of Bologna. Here, the ponies were stabled in a high-class establishment while I slept in the back of the horse truck.

"We are stressed and we know where we are going. You are calm and don't know where you are going!" said Kiriakos, with the help of Alex, acting as translator.

"Well, I have to trust God!" I replied decisively. He was all the security I had – for here I was, plunged into another foreign country, with no map, no Italian mobile phone, and just a few Italian words scribbled on paper. All I knew was that I was going north to Monte Bianco and the Alps, and then into France to rest my ponies with my friend Ali, near Geneva.

"We thought you would be a bit strange, but you are actually quite nice," Alex admitted when they said goodbye, and her compliment made me smile. I was feeling quite lonely and missing my Greek companions when a trim, elderly gentleman approached on a bay horse and enquired in English where I was from and where I was going.

"I'm from England, but just arrived from Greece, and we are going North. I need a map to help me get there," I replied, and he offered me a lift into town.

"I saved them," he said, pointing to his horse and dog and making a cutthroat sign, reminding me that people eat horse meat in Italy. He introduced himself as Mauro Checcoli. "I am quite famous around these parts as I've won several gold medals, including one at the Tokyo Olympics in 1964," he said, adding: "If you need anything give me a call." He gave me his phone number.

I spent two hours criss-crossing the town, struggling with the new language, with people pointing me in different directions. I was very hot by the end, but at least I now had a map and an Italian sim card in my phone.

ITALY – ITALIA

20. Complimenti

"Why is it so hot?" I asked. I was disappointed – I'd presumed that Italy would be cooler, being that much further north than Greece. If anything, it was worse, as this was not dry heat but much more humid – I later learnt that Italy was in the midst of a heat wave. Using my few words of Italian, I got a taxi back to the stables where I tried to have a siesta until it cooled off. I lay on my bedroll behind the stables, while my ponies grazed, but flying insects kept landing on me. I covered myself with my silk sleeping bag liner, but this prevented the breeze from cooling me. By four o'clock, I gave up my siesta, packed up and left. Somehow, using my new map, I needed to find a way around the huge city of Bologna, which sprawled before me.

Travelling on the busy roads on the outskirts of the city, I was pleased to find that Italian drivers were more polite. "Bravo! Complimenti! Buono!" they exclaimed enthusiastically, giving me the thumbs up – they were clearly a demonstrative people. But when I asked the way to Monte Carlo, one woman waved me back in the direction I had come and another man told me to keep going. I decided to go forwards and wound up and down until I joined another busy main road. A man dressed in a broad red and white striped jersey and a red cap was shouting at me, and I guessed he was asking me where I was going. "Sasso Marconi," I shouted back. He motioned for me to follow him along a track through a park, and disappeared and then reappeared as he directed me through a complicated road system, which didn't appear on my map.

After guiding me through this big urban sprawl he pointed towards Sasso Marconi – named after Guglielmo Marconi, the radio pioneer who received the first transatlantic radio signal in 1902, at Poldhu Cove, in Cornwall, England. "Ciao!" he waved. "Grazie!" I shouted back over the noise of the traffic, and once again we were alone on a winding uphill road, competing with trucks and heavy traffic. Although both ponies and I wore fluorescent strips, I didn't want to be on busy roads at dusk, so I was praying to find a safe place to camp, with grass and trees to tether the ponies. Everywhere I looked there were walls and high fences, containing ferocious guard dogs, and with security signs and intercoms at every entrance.

I was scanning the sides of the road when I spotted a wide grassy verge hidden by bushes. I urged the ponies through a gap and onto the grass, and despite being scratched by brambles, I pressed through the thick hedges until I found some sturdy branches to attach the long tethering ropes. Then I unsaddled them and rolled out my bedroll between them. I lay there, looking up at the stars and moon in the welcome coolness of the night, wearing earplugs to muffle the sound of passing traffic, changing gear on the hill just the other side of the hedge.

I left when it was safe and light enough for the traffic to see us, but as the sun rose, so did the heat and the hot road burnt my soles and the softer skin under my toes. My strength evaporated from my body, and by midday it was almost unbearable. As I stopped to buy a snack in one town, my sunglasses fell off and were trodden on. I carried on my way, with both lenses taped into place in broken frames. I had no choice – when I'd previously ridden without sunglasses, the bright sun made my eyes and head ache. To add to my desperation, I saw a sign saying 10km to Bologna – we'd spent ten hot hours skirting the southern edge of the city, and were still on the outskirts.

Claudio Gambarini and Anna Maria Gratia.

I was continuing along a busy street when a man and a woman ran alongside us, talking Italian enthusiastically. When they saw I didn't understand, they tried some English, and I realised the woman was inviting me to visit her sister at riding stables on the edge of town.

I backtracked, following their directions, and was welcomed by Anna Maria, who helped me unsaddle and gave water and hay to the ponies.

"You are a woman. Don't forget!" she said, offering me a shower, and this was followed by lunch with her husband Claudio. Afterwards, he let me use his computer to check my emails, but I couldn't even find the '@' sign on his Italian keyboard to sign in and he didn't understand, so he called an English-speaking friend, who explained – it made both of us laugh.

"My husband Claudio has a big heart!" said Anna Maria with a smile. Everyone was keen to help, including her sister Elizabetha and her husband, Stephano – the couple who had directed me to the stables.

"It is so hot maybe you should get a lift to where it is cooler – it would be kinder to your ponies too," suggested Anna Maria. "You could go west to France, to avoid the mountains in the north." They were all so hospitable and fed me delicious food including pizza and Italian ice cream.

21. Circolo Ippico Caledonia

How can we understand the road we travel? It is the Lord who directs our steps.
Proverbs 20v24 NLT

"You can't move your ponies in Italy if you don't have a Coggins test," warned Anna Maria. "And you can't visit any riding stables – if your ponies haven't been tested, they could be closed down."

Neither the Greek vets nor the international horse transporter had said anything about the need for a coggins blood test in Italy, and I was worried that I could get these kind people into serious trouble. Anna Maria suggested I speak to a man who was delivering grain, whose name was Elia Buoncuore. He unfolded a map of the area and proceeded to give me directions in flowing Italian, which sounded lovely, but I didn't understand a word. After a while, he realised, chatted to someone on his phone, and then handed it to me.

"I hear you're in a spot of trouble?" said a woman with a broad Scottish accent, taking me completely by surprise. She introduced herself as Moira and I explained the problem. "Yes, of course I can help you – come over here!"

After their evening riding lessons, Stephano and Elizabeth kindly gave us a lift west to Moira Barron and Elia Buoncuore's stables, called Circolo Ippico Caledonia (Riding Club Caledonia - the Latin name for Scotland). It was situated near Qualtro Castella (cabbage mountain) in Reggio Emilia. Moira said she'd come to live in Italy after working with horses in Ibiza, Spain.

"I find teaching very satisfying," she told me, as she gave riding lessons to a group of teenagers. "These girls are very good, and they even do the mucking out!"

Moira was my heroine, and helped me on every front. After her lessons, and before it got too hot she took me to a veterinary department, where I learnt that I needed an important pink slip of paper. We were told we then needed to go to another department, in another town, to have the papers inspected. Later that day a vet visited and took blood samples from the ponies.

"Now we have to go to the Emilia regional authorities to get the passports checked," stated Moira. When we got there, everyone seemed confused by the Greek passports, which didn't have the right reference number for Greece, and had the wrong gender for the ponies.

"All of this should have been sorted out in Greece," said Moira translating, adding in exasperation: "To get these papers I'll have to register your ponies in my name. But I will sell them back to you when you get to England, as I have already plenty of ponies at home!"

There were more problems: "There's nothing here to say they are not for human consumption," Moira added. "In every European country, passports must have a page to say the horse is not for butchering. This piece of paper will cost you a further sixty six Euros each pony!"

"After all of this, they'd be much too expensive to eat!" I joked, trying to use humour to cope with my exasperation – I found all of this bureaucracy unbelievable.

"If you don't get the right paperwork within a certain time, they will fine you," warned Moira.

Another vet came to check the ponies, and asked: "Is this one grey or is she...?" Both Moira and I jumped in with a quick "Si!". We were not going to allow him to question her colour and create yet more problems. I'd waited nine days in Greece to get the necessary paperwork, and after another week in Italy I finally had the Coggins test, a pink slip of paper, and another to say the ponies were not for eating. I couldn't have managed without Moira's incredible help to make sure the ponies were law-abiding travellers in Italy.

"You know, the bureaucracy in Italy isn't just for horses, it's for everything," she said. However romantic the country was, I was glad I didn't live here and have to deal with this on a daily basis.

Moira kindly took me to meet a man called Titzano, who led horse treks through the Alps. He showed us some maps and, with Moira as translator, I picked up some useful tips on the terrain and where I could camp with the ponies in the mountains.

Moira then took me sightseeing. I was struck by the emptiness of the landscape – totally devoid of animals, which were kept inside. Here and there, I saw big, round bales – sometimes just one or two perched on a small corner of land, which we wouldn't consider big enough to make hay in England. They seemed to make the most of every corner of every field here in Quatro Castella, where castles were perched on hilltops.

Moira Barron, Beatrice and Eleia Buoncuore

70

Quatro Castella, where castles were perched on hill tops.

Moira Barron

The kindness of strangers

I would have liked to see Tuscany, but the Alps beckoned me, and my enthusiasm evaporated in the 35 to 45 degree heatwave and the 80% humidity – even my little Greek horses felt it. Italy had a romantic aura, with its poetic language, historic buildings, vineyards and olive groves. However, the idea of dragging the ponies through traffic and car fumes, and plodding across the several hundred miles of sweltering plains between us and the Alps seemed far from romantic!

"Have you given the ponies enough hay?" asked Moira and Elia. They were intent on feeding my ponies up, especially Ermis whose ribs had been noticeable ever since I first met him in Greece.

My prayer that their shoes would last supernaturally over five weeks across Greece had been answered. Yoana had just one loose shoe, which Moira's farrier easily reset.

Moira was dedicated to getting me and my ponies sorted for the next section of our journey. She offered me a comfortable leather saddle, which fitted Yoana but not Ermis, with his narrow back. She also gave me the most lush, woollen seat saver, which became one of my luxuries, along with a canvas fold-up bucket – another treasure, as I could tuck it into the pack. It was so much better than my awkward red one, hanging off the edge of the pack, which had been squashed between the ponies, my knees and against walls, and was now cracked.

Yoana diving for grass as was her habit!

With the helpful girls at Franco Pitti's Circolo Ippico San Maurizio.

Moira also gave me another bridle with a snaffle bit for the pack pony, as whenever Yoana made a dive for the grass, she pulled Ermis and me with her. This, combined with Ermis' habit of stopping abruptly whenever he did droppings, had given me rope burns on my stomach and worn holes in my gloves. Although Ermis was the smaller of the two, he had a much bigger head, so we had to punch several more holes in the bridle. I tried schooling them in the arena at Circolo Ippico Caledonia, but they opened their mouths – it was clear they'd never been schooled in their lives – so Moira also gave me a grackle noseband to keep their mouths shut.

There were only a few things left to buy: a breastplate, a cropper to keep the saddle in place when climbing mountains and a cheap pair of sunglasses (although I found they made my eyes ache). Then Moira and her assistant Kayleigh took me to a camera shop to buy an attachment for my tripod and a new camera case, so that I could carry it over the front of the saddle.

"The sad thing is that you have everything now," Moira remarked, as we left the shop. "And now… more adventures."

"I couldn't have done without your amazing help Moira," I replied. "The day I met Elia was God's perfect timing!"

"I didn't believe before, but it does make me think," she added.

Elia thought I should stay longer to learn more Italian, but I needed to press on. The hottest time of the year was approaching, and we needed to keep going north to the Alps. They refused to take any payment for the ponies or my keep, and Moira kept offering me more useful things, including a wind-up torch, a hoof pick, a compass and an Italian magazine containing a map of Monte Bianco.

" You had better use this and the compass!" she warned me, in her good-humoured Scottish way, before arranging a lift across the plains in a trailer – saving us a two-week, intense slog in intense heat, through heavy traffic. I was sad to leave, but excited to see the Alps, with remnants of snow on the peaks, rising steeply into the sky like a wall hanging.

Unusually, I'd booked some stables in advance, as I needed to get some local directions. These very smart riding school grounds looked wintry, as the leaves had been stripped from the trees by a hailstorm the previous week. The owner wasn't friendly, and I wished I'd decided to camp in the countryside.

"Get the ponies in. The flies are bothering them," she ordered, just as they were enjoying some grass. "You have too much stuff," she complained. I replied that the pack was actually lighter than me – it just looked big with the foam bedroll on top. I then asked her for some basic directions.

"No, I don't have time," she replied. Her young assistant was much more friendly, but was unable to help. She looked at me camping outside, and remarked: "Your ponies cost more to stable than you do!"

I missed Moira and her friendly crew, and was glad to leave these stables, even though I didn't have a detailed map and no idea where I was heading. I asked several people en route, but was confused by their Italian directions and got completely lost. It was an exasperating start to a new day, but at least the climate this far north made getting lost more bearable.

22. Piano piano!

After a lot of guesswork, I found my way to the main road. This led to a dark tunnel, so I hoped a track beside the road would allow me to avoid it. I was relieved to find that it did. Half a mile later, we were back on the main road… only to face our next challenge: a narrow viaduct with tall railings on either side. I was grateful that the truck drivers were patient, and once we were over the bridge, I took the first turning off the busy road. I hoped it would somehow take us in the right direction, even if it meant a lot of wiggling around.

We stopped at a village water fountain. The water continuously flowed out of a lion's mouth and into a stone trough, and the ponies were not happy to find that they couldn't drink without getting their heads wet. Seeing our predicament, a man kindly plugged the holes with sticks. While they drank, a cyclist came to fill his water bottle and told me to continue on this road through Laurange and Fiorano to Lessolo, which I jotted down on paper so as to not forget. When I reached Fiorano, I was taking some photos, while dogs were madly barking, and wondering where to go next, when an Italian couple hailed me from a balcony.

"Dove Lessolo per favore?" (where is Lessolo please?) I shouted back over the din of the dogs. Within minutes the man appeared with a bicycle, and escorted us through the winding streets and then along a muddy wooded track. By the time he left me, I'd lost my bearings, and another complicated road system lay ahead. I was pondering what to do. I needed to get to a riding stables in Borgofranco because Moira had sent my tripod I had forgotten there, but I knew that if I called Monica, my contact at the stables, I wouldn't understand her Italian directions.

"Oh God, I'm stuck again!" I said. "It's so difficult not speaking Italian. What am I going to do?"

"Tracey!" someone called out. I thought I'd imagined it, but then I saw a man on a bicycle, and recognised Dario Della Rina, who had helped me with directions at the water fountain earlier.

"Thank God you turned up!" I exclaimed. "How do I get to the Circolo Ippico San Maurizio, in Borgofranco?" He called the stables on my behalf and then guided me there through a complicated set of roadworks. He often had to wait for us, which showed how slow we really were!

"Piano, piano (softly, softly)!" he said with a smile, adding proudly: "We have just passed Ivrea, where the typewriter was invented by Camillo Olivetti." Eventually we arrived at the stables, to find that the tripod had arrived earlier, but had been sent back because it wasn't expected. After I'd said goodbye to Dario, I called Moira and asked her to speak Italian to Monica about the tripod.

An English-speaking lady then informed me: "The owner, Franco Pitti, likes what you are doing and said there was no charge for you staying in the clubhouse or for your ponies either!" How welcome that was after everything I had just been through. Now I could relax, and sleep on my bedroll on the clubhouse floor, beneath a dramatic photograph of horses and riders in front of mountains – I guessed that Franco Pitti must be a long distance rider himself.

The next day was Saturday, and after another failed attempt to trace my tripod, I continued towards Pont Saint Martin, hoping to buy a map of the Vallé d'Aosta and the Swiss Alps before everything closed the following day.

Lost in an Italian village!

Dario Della Rina & the fountain man.

23. Pont St. Martin

Security is a myth - it doesn't exist.
Life is either a daring adventure or nothing at all. - Helen Keller

I followed the back roads, winding between the villages, but as the valley narrowed, and the vineyards which cloaked its steep walls were replaced by a mountain rock face, I was forced to rejoin the main road.

In Pont St. Martin, I found the tourist information centre, and parked my Greek horses in a car space marked 'private'. They did a good job of trimming the overgrown verge, while I enquired about routes to the Alps and Monte Bianco. The tourist information people were extremely helpful, giving me advice on how to travel through Parco Naturale del Mont Avic. Meanwhile a man brought buckets of water for the ponies.

I asked if I could use their loo. "Yes we do have a bathroom downstairs. We're not insured for you to use it, but we will make an exception to you. Be careful!" the lady warned me, and I gingerly stepped down the stairs, smiling at how 'careful' western society had become. If only these people knew that insurance companies considered me too much of a risk, and refused to insure me! Anyway, I had the biggest insurer of all time – Almighty God and His angels – so we were in good hands!

As I was winding the tethering ropes around the ponies' necks, a car pulled up and a woman with intense, bright blue eyes started talking to me in Italian, before switching to English and telling me her name was Barbara.

"We have horses, just over there," she said, pointing. A tall, dark man stepped out of the car, and she introduced him as Paolo. "Bring your horses – Paolo will show you the way."

I rode off and Paolo cycled to meet me – my fourth Italian guide on a bicycle! He didn't speak English, but used hand signals to show me to an old house and barn, where Barbara was waiting. They took me to a cellar with a low ceiling, with a room full of saddles and harness, meticulously arranged. Barbara told me that horses were Paolo's passion, as he paraded his matching Gelderlanders, which he drove as a pair, with a large wagon, in the local festival every year. She also showed me her pretty, yellow dun pony.

"Paolo has a very understanding wife!" added Barbara, and invited me to stay at Paolo's house, promising me a shower and Italian pizza and wine.

"I have four horses at the door of my house. They are very quiet and stick together," Paolo told me, with Barbara's help, and I worked out what he meant as we drove through the electric gates, which were decorated with the silhouettes of four horses. Barbara told me she'd learnt English in Exeter, close to my home in Devon, south west England. At the house I met Paolo's wife, Serena, and their ten-year-old son, Jacopo, who was as tall as me, at five foot five!

Paolo leaving the ponies from his bicycle and with one of his Gelderlanders.

24. Aosta Valley

The narrow, rugged Aosta Valley is crowded with medieval buildings. It has been an important historical, political, geographical and commercial route for centuries, bringing much wealth to the local noble families, who created many artistic masterpieces. Signals could be sent over several hundred miles, from Torino to Martigny in France, using a series of towers, with flags by day and fires by night.

The following morning I set off past the fortified Verres Castle, which has stood high on its defensive, rocky summit since Medieval times. My willing photographic team, consisting of new-found friends Paolo, Jacopo and Mattius, caught up with me here and took both photos and film of me and the ponies. I knew the photos had come out well, because I could see them on the back of my camera, but I was less sure about the video, which had been filmed from the back of a moving vehicle, bumping along the cobbled roads! I tried to explain that I wanted to see the scenery as well as the ponies, but it was a challenge, especially without being able to speak Italian!

25. Forte di Bard

I passed several castles in the Aosta Valley, including Forte di Bard – the most dramatic fortification, built to guard the entrance to the valley and used since the 6th century to control the route between Italy and France. From the 10th century, the castle was under control of the powerful lords of Bard, but ownership passed to the House of Savoy in the middle of the 13th century, when the defences were fortified further still.

In 1800, 400 soldiers were garrisoned here, and managed to hold Napoleon's 40,000-strong army at bay for two weeks, ruining his plan of making a surprise attack on the Po Valley and Turin. He ordered the fort to be destroyed, and it wasn't rebuilt until 1830. Charles Albert Savoy, fearing new attacks from the French, spent eight years reconstructing the fort on two levels – the upper part with conventional battlements, and the lower part with 50 gun ports.

By the end of the 19th century, the fort was only used as a gunpowder store by the Italian army. Today, it houses the Museum of the Alps.

Crossing the bridge at Bard.

Go confidently in the direction of your dreams. Live the life you have imagined. – Henry David Thoreau

26.
Val di Champorcher

Paolo drove us up a steep mountain, around hairpin bends, to Champorcher, where I was invited to lunch with Serena's mother and sister. Afterwards, I set off with the ponies, sharing a track with four-wheel drives and walkers. However crowded, it felt good to be up in the mountains and out of the roads and towns crammed into the valley below.

I felt warm as I climbed, leading the ponies, but quickly cooled down when I stopped to take photos. We moved above the treeline and arrived at the Refugio Dondena – a cold, windswept spot, at 2,000 metres, with far-reaching views. Paolo had kindly arranged for both my ponies and me to stay here. As I sat by the fire, it was hard to believe that only a few hundred miles to the south, the climate was too hot to bear!

Paolo arrived later and we ate a delicious starter of dried meat and marinated nuts, followed by polenta (ground maize) and tasty sausages. At the end, Loris, the landlord, brought out his mother's genepy liqueur, flavoured by mountain flowers.

Left: Refugio Dondena situated by the Parco Naturale del Monte Avic and above: The Vicario family.

27. Mountain climbing

In the morning I mended one of the pack panniers, which had been ripped on the Bard Bridge the previous day. As I was following the track, my daydreaming was interrupted when I noticed that Ermis was no longer attached to Yoana, but was walking off in the opposite direction. When I rushed after him, he started to trot.

"Where are you going this time Ermis?" I asked – he always had an urge to turn back. "Your new home is in England and that way is forward!"

There was another sudden interruption to my daydreaming when a cyclist screeched to a halt on a rough track above us, causing the ponies to spin around in fright. From then on I had to concentrate carefully, leading the ponies up along narrow tracks, over boulder-strewn mountainsides.

As we neared the summit, the rough path became so rocky and steep that there was no place even to stop for a breather, and I had to keep the momentum going. My Greek ponies were not accustomed to climbing mountains, so I was praying we wouldn't fall off the narrow path. By the time we reached the Tour de Pouton saddle (3,000 metres), they were gasping for breath, with nostrils dilating and heaving flanks. The bitter, cold wind at the top soon cooled us down, so we didn't linger.

The descent looked so steep, it made me gulp, and I continued praying until we'd descended the first 50 metres, and the path became smoother. At the bottom we were greeted by a friendly flock of goats and sheep, who approached us inquisitively until Yoana laid her ears back at them, causing them to scatter.

It was cold, so we pressed on, but somehow I missed the Refugio Sogno, which I'd been told was horse friendly. Feeling exhausted, I found a grassy spot on a terrace overlooking Lilaz in the valley beneath us. After a very cold night, I was up at 6am and was glad to be packing and warming up. Once we arrived on the valley floor, we followed a path along the Cogne River.

To avoid the main road, I took a path which climbed steeply up the other side of the mountain and ended up in a huge boulder field, which was too dangerous for the ponies to cross, as they could break a leg. So we backtracked down the mountain, arrived back at the same place we'd been three hours earlier and rejoined the main road. My reward for this diversion was to see three Bouquetin (Capri ibex), which are mainly found in the Alps. They were widespread until the 15th century, but were almost wiped out following the introduction of firearms. The breed was saved by the Italian monarchs, who prohibited hunting on their land.

28. Alpine tunnels

Facing it - always facing it, that's the way to get through.
Face it. – Joseph Conrad

Our next obstacles were dark tunnels. The first time I reached one, I hoped someone would stop and offer me an escort, complete with flashing lights, but no one did. So I unpacked my own flashing head torch and dressed us up in yellow fluorescents. One tunnel followed another and each time I would pray our way through the darkness.

Before descending into the built-up area around Aymavilles, I found a place to camp that was off the road and above the town, hidden by some trees. I was so tired and stiff from climbing up and down mountains that I was on my bedroll before dusk. I even noticed Yoana lying down after she'd had her fill of grass. I rarely saw Ermis lying down.

The following morning was overcast. I was following a minor road up the Aosta valley when a truck beeped its horn behind me. "I can't get any closer to the side of the road!" I thought to myself. After overtaking, the truck stopped in front of us and out jumped Paolo, offering me a chocolate croissant and a bottle of water! Using sign language, I indicated that my phone battery was flat, and I had no way of finding out what had happened to my tripod. Somehow he understood, and used his own phone to call Monica, and then Marco, her English-speaking boyfriend, who explained that the tripod had arrived. He also told me there was a place for my ponies to spend the night further up the Aosta Valley in Derby.

Paolo drove off in his truck with my phone to charge it, and by the time he returned, an hour later, it had begun to drizzle. This was the first time it had rained since Greece, when it had helped to cool me down. I didn't need it here, for even though it was July, it wasn't hot in the Italian mountain valleys. Paolo gave me my phone back, and also a large yellow mac. I'd mislaid my coat in Greece and only bought a small replacement, but this one was so big that it kept me, my saddle and camera dry.

He showed me the best route on the map, and suggested ways to avoid the tunnels. I later found out that some of these routes had been blocked off with concrete slabs. I hoped they might be the fake, polystyrene slabs that you see on the movies, and tried to move them, but they wouldn't budge! Travelling down the main roads was stressful enough, but in the tunnels, we also had to deal with the amplified echoes of the vehicles, which perturbed me more than the ponies. There wasn't much space, and there were big logging trucks on the road, so I prayed that none would pass through the tunnel at the same time as we did. I was grateful that none did.

Paolo arrived in a truck with coffee and a chocolate croissant!

29. Determination – Val Ferret

"L'avventura è dentro di noi." The adventure is inside us." Walter Bonatti

I was greeted at Derby by Katia, Marco's friend, with the offer of an overnight paddock. There I met her husband Sandro, who gave me a bale of hay, refused to take any payment and kindly invited me to stay in their little apartment.

Yoana had a loose shoe, so they directed me to a riding stable at Morgex, where I used sign language to (eventually) explain that I needed some nail tighteners. As I struggled to use them, the owner Alberto Borrovellhio took over from me, gave the ponies hay and said I must rest them. Then it was my turn to eat: "A party for you!" said an English-speaking girl called Victoria, as sandwiches arrived.

"It is impossible – wonder woman!" exclaimed Alberto, after I'd told him my story. This made me smile, remembering my attempts to move concrete slabs the previous day! "Please wait, wait," he pleaded, as I started to pack up the ponies. "You can go after coffee. Italian coffee!" Victoria even invited me to stay the night, and I was tempted, but Marco had booked me in at a 'refugio' up the Val Ferret.

I continued on to Courmayeur, where I tied the ponies to a tree in front of the tourist information office. I expected the staff to be as helpful as they'd been in Pont St. Martin, but "no" seemed to be the general answer: "No you can't do that." "No we don't have maps." "No you can't take your horses into town unless you ask the police." So I carried on anyway until I spotted a church and another convenient tree, away from the crowds. I tied the ponies here while I ran up to the shops to buy a map of Mont Blanc and some food supplies.

As I left Courmayeur, a huge articulated lorry passed us, with DETERMINATION boldly written down the side… not once, but twice. It was uncanny – this was definitely a message for me, not only for this journey, but for my life. I needed it today, as I'd been told it was only six kilometres to the refugio, but it was much longer and the stony track was steep. We were hot and tired by the time we arrived, after dark, at this exposed site – I'd have preferred to camp in the valley, where it was sheltered and there was more grass. Some young men helped me with my pack and, after soup, I slept in a large dormitory, where there were lots of bodies and no fresh air. I longed to be in my tent with my ponies grazing nearby. But in the morning it was all worthwhile.

"This is the first time in two weeks that you can see Monte Bianco!" said a young man called Remy. I asked him to take photos of us with the mountain in the background, and directed him carefully, but had to return several times to check the picture – it was a shot that we had to get right!

"I have taken about a hundred!" he exclaimed. "I really need to get back to work now." Before I left, I thanked his boss for allowing him to help me. Even before reaching the Alps, I'd had a feeling that I'd be given an opportunity to photograph Monte Bianco, and that this would be on the front cover of my book.

Before I left, I asked Remy to translate one of the quotes on the wall of the refugio. "It is true of you!" he replied. "L'avventura è dentro di noi – the adventure is inside us."

Life is not measured by the number of breaths we take, but the moments that take our breath away.
– Hilary Cooper

I ambled through the spectacular scenery, pausing for photographs.

"Ermis, there is no grass back at the refugio!" I reminded him as he started heading back yet again, even though we were surrounded by lush, mountain pastures. I had to attach him to Yoana.

Everything was so pleasant on our descent back into the Val Ferret, until some runners suddenly appeared and the ponies took off down a steep slope. I tried to hold on, but they were moving unusually fast, and I was almost flying between them.

Instinct told me to let go at the moment they were slightly apart, so that they wouldn't trample me when I hit the ground, but the speed and impact was so great that all the breath was knocked out of me, and I bashed my right knee hard again. I quickly gulped some air back into my lungs, scrambled to my feet and hobbled after them. The French couple who had frightened them asked if it was their fault.

"Si!" I replied, but they simply continued on their run, which surprised me – I presumed they'd help me find my ponies, of which there was no sign.

I was thankful no one had been coming up the rough path when the ponies were careering down as they could have been knocked over. I anxiously looked for hoof marks on the dirt path, but in my rush, I descended too far down the mountain and turned to climb back up.

"God, I hope they are okay," I prayed. I rounded the next bend, and there they were! They trotted towards me and stopped. "Thank you Jesus!" I exclaimed.

I checked them over and discovered they were fine, and the pack and camera were still all in place. Relieved, I continued limping down the mountain to the Chalet Val Ferret where I was expected, thanks to a phone call from helpful tourist information ladies at Pont St. Martin. There I tethered them on a grassy lawn.

The super helpful Paolo arrived early the next morning with a boot full of goodies for us all, including a generous supply of food for the ponies – I very much regretted that I couldn't carry it all. He also gave me my famous tripod, which I'd left at Moira's. She'd sent it on to Monica in Borgo Franco, but they didn't know it was for me, so the delivery had not been accepted. I'd then lost track of it for a week, until Paolo collected it.

After the ponies had devoured their breakfast, Paolo accompanied us a little way up the mountain and took more photos before we parted company. I continued until we reached a small footbridge, which was too narrow for Yoana and her pack, so I had to unload everything and drag it across. It was so narrow and steep on the other side that it was very tricky to reload, which caused a traffic jam of walkers, all intent on reaching the summit. Some barged past, while others waited patiently, and one couple kindly helped me pack. Later on, this same couple caught up with me, further up the mountain, and handed me my tripod – I hadn't noticed that it had dropped out of the pack!

30. Colle del Grand Ferret

A big achievement is made up of little steps - Robert Schuller

I led the ponies up the mountain track, which continued to get steeper. We got into a rhythm, which involved taking a number of steps and then stopping to catch our breath. Sometimes the rest spots were chosen by Yoana and sometimes by me. A dozen or so steps and then rest, another dozen, and another rest… until we finally reached Col Grand Ferret, on the border between Italy and Switzerland.

Above: Still in Italy but near the top with the glaciers behind us.
I led the ponies up the steep mountain from Val Ferret but mounted for this photo on the right!

SWITZERLAND – LA SUISSE

31. Tour du Mont Blanc

The descent from over 2,500 metres (8,200ft) was less abrupt than the ascent, and I enjoyed the more gentle path down into the wide glacial valley – curved like the hull of a boat. But along with the sudden change of scenery came a change of language: with every encounter I said "ciao" or "buongiorno" and everyone replied "bonjour". Just as I'd begun to grasp some words of Italian, I now had to reach deep into my mind to find distant memories of my school French.

I continued along the Tour du Mont Blanc (TMB) trail in the drizzle, until I found a grassy spot off the track, hidden among some trees. I gave the ponies some food that Paolo had provided, which they relished. I couldn't resist giving them more, as it had been a huge day of mountain climbing and I was sure that if my legs were aching, then theirs must be too. I was thankful for the big yellow mac and the tarpaulin that Paolo had also given to me, very thoughtfully, along with many goodies. Usually my diet consisted of tuna, pasta, nuts and dried fruit, which was fine, but got boring. Paolo had provided small tins of tuna, delicious pâté and Italian cake.

By nine I was tucked up in my sleeping bag, but at half past ten I was woken up by shots – sometimes so frequent they sounded like machine gun fire. I was concerned that hunters were getting close to us, so I scrambled to pull on some clothes and to find the fluorescent vests, which I fastened around the ponies' necks to make them more visible in the dark.

For he orders his angels to protect you wherever you go.

They will steady you with their hands to keep you from stumbling against the rocks on the trail. Psalm 91v11 TLB

I was packed up and away by seven in the morning, as I knew I had to get along the track before competing for space with all the Sunday walkers. At one point, it became so narrow that there was a chain attached to the mountainside for walkers to hold on to. This made me nervous – Yoana, with her pack, was three times the width of a person. The drop on the other side was so scary that I really had to control my fears as she scraped her way along the stony wall. When a stone bounced down from above and startled the ponies, I held my breath, praying that they wouldn't fall.

We made good progress to Champex, past people fishing in the lake, and here I bought a large, tasty brown roll, which took me several days to finish, accompanied by tuna or pâté. As I was preparing to leave, a little boy became transfixed by the ponies, and didn't even hear his father calling him. I tried to speak to them in French, but they didn't appear to understand, so I just gave them a big international smile.

Yoana's front shoe was sounding loose on the road. I didn't like to hear this, knowing it would be tricky to find a farrier in this part of Switzerland, so I just carried on – hoping her shoes would stay on in the same supernatural way as they had in Greece. I just needed to get to my friend Ali's place over the mountains in France.

At Champex d'en Haut, I unpacked the ponies and tethered them out to graze. I had to tie Yoana away from Ermis, as she always wanted to hog all the grass. A man kindly pointed the track out to me and although he only spoke in French, I got the gist of what he was telling me: that the mountain was steep and not good for horses. I hoped he was exaggerating, but I became concerned when the guide book confirmed that it was very steep and stony.

After Plan de L'Au, the path began to get rougher, but I thought it was passable… until we arrived at a small gate in front of a four-foot rock face. I roped the gate back, untacked the ponies so their saddlery wouldn't get caught in tree roots or the gate, and hauled the packs up by hand. Then it was the ponies' turn. Ermis looked at me as if to say, "you're not asking me to climb up there, are you?" With encouragement he did follow me, slipping and sliding on the rocks. Once I'd tied him at the top, I returned for Yoana who followed eagerly, not wanting to get left behind.

I believe that we can do it – so we can do it.
– Albert in the film War Horse

Once we were up and over the steep slope, I had to repack, which took half an hour in the confines of the narrow, muddy track. Only a little further on, we found ourselves in a maze of sheer rocks, which surrounded us. Yoana refused to continue, and there was no space to squeeze Ermis in front. We were stuck! Eventually I managed to force Ermis past Yoana, and he plunged forwards. I hurried ahead up the slope, trying to maintain momentum, and he followed me. Yoana was anxious not to get left behind, so I quickly returned for her, but she found no grip on the rock and kept slipping backwards.

"Help Jesus! Angels!" I called – it was all I could find to say.

"Go back!" warned some walkers, who were heading down the slope, but they didn't know that going down slippery boulders was more dangerous than going up. Retreat was impossible. I had no choice but to advance up the mountain, continually off-loading, dragging the packs up, returning for Ermis, who was more surefooted with his smaller hooves, and then going back for Yoana. Then I would repack, until we reached the next dangerously steep portion of track. At one point, I left Yoana to follow… but never again. She went the wrong side of a tree and stopped right at the edge of a mountain cliff. I quickly attached Ermis to a tree in case he followed me, scrambled to the cliff edge and coaxed her to walk backwards.

"DETERMINATION." I remembered that word, on a truck in Italy, and I really needed it now. I had no choice but to believe and persist. I knew that after all this going up, we would have to come down, and I just hoped the descent would be easier than the ascent. On one narrow rocky section, where there was no other way to go, Yoana got her hoof caught in a narrow groove. She pulled back, but I pleaded and coaxed her on and up to where Ermis was waiting.

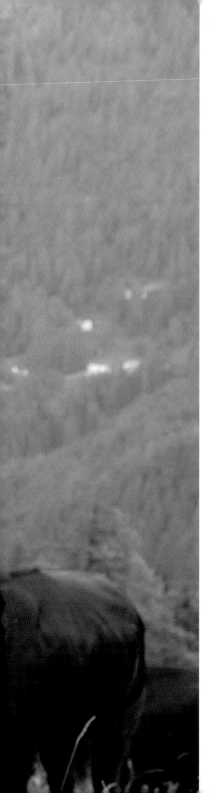

32. Fighting Queens

Although the light was fading, the trees were thinning out and I could see more sky, which gave me hope. Also, I could hear a melody of cow bells, which meant there was open ground above. But when we got there, we startled a herd of cows and made them charge off. I prayed that they wouldn't stampede over a cliff, but they soon returned, particularly the older cows, who were the most curious.

I recognised them to be 'Fighting Queens' (the Herens breed), with their thick Swiss collars and heavy bells – an awesome sight against the grand mountain backdrop. The cows traditionally take part in 'combats de reines' (queen fights), a century-old spectator sport. The breed naturally fights to determine dominance and grazing rights in the herd, by pushing their foreheads together, and the one that doesn't back down is the 'queen'. Unlike the bloody Spanish bull fights, the overall winner is called 'the queen of queens' and is treated like royalty. Each year a grand final is held in Martigny where the best from seven districts compete in six weight categories – the largest can weigh over 700kg (more than two thirds of a ton)!

I stopped day dreaming when I got a shock from the electric fence. There was no gateway for my ponies but fortunately the battery pack wasn't far away, so I switched it off and hurriedly took the fence down to get my ponies over, before rushing back to turn it back on before any of the majestic beasts could escape.

33. The European Alps

The climb had taken twice as long as I'd anticipated, and by the time we reached the dramatic, open mountainside, it was dusk and rapidly cooling off. I quickly captured some photos of the awesome scenery before pressing on up the mountain, leading the ponies with urgency – we needed to find shelter and a grassy campsite before the darkness moved in like a blanket. We arrived at a gate leading to a steep drop into the adjoining valley, so I tied the ponies to it and scouted the area, looking for grass, shelter and enough flat ground to lie down. There was nothing suitable, so I hurriedly unpacked, slipping and sliding on the slope, and pitched the tent on the most level ground I could find.

Your love, O Lord, reaches to the heavens, Your faithfulness to the skies. Your righteousness is like the mighty mountains, Your justice like the great deep. O Lord, You preserve both man and beast. Psalm 36v5-6 NIV

The tent was still damp from the previous night. I shivered as I remembered the heat of Greece and southern Italy, and was grateful for Paolo's extra coat. Once again, I was alerted by distant shots and scrambled out of the tent to see that the sounds were coming from a firework display, far below in the valley, in the direction of Martigny. I chuckled at myself, realising that the 'gunfire' I'd heard on the previous night must also have been fireworks, celebrating Swiss National Day on the first of August!

Blessed are those who laugh at themselves, for they shall never cease to be amused.

34. Col de la Forclaz

The following morning, as I scrambled to pack up on the slippery slope, I discovered I'd left the pack too close to Ermis and he had pooped on the bridles! We left our camp at seven, in warming sunshine, and dropped down into the shade of the mountain, passing a farm at Bovine, with smoke curling out of its chimney. It was so cool here, even on the first of August.

At the Col de la Forclaz, which was buzzing with tourists, I stopped in the sunshine to warm up and eat some of the bread and cheese I'd bought the previous day. I washed it down with an expensive bottle of water, costing the equivalent of £4, from the local souvenir shop… and then found a pipe leading into a water trough where I refilled it for free! While I was there, I met a couple who bred quarter horses in Texas and a French man who had followed the old Camino de Santiago pilgrim trail with his two donkeys.

Leaving our resting place, we followed the path, found our way past a barricade and reached the bottom, only to find that it ended with a steep, curving staircase down to the road. I groaned, thinking we'd have to climb all the way back to the Col. It was completely unsuitable for horses, but I coaxed Yoana down the steps, scraping the packs along the curved wall. Ermis decided he had a better idea and I held my breath as he leapt off the four foot wall, straight onto the main road!

FRANCE – LA FRANCE

35. Col de Balme

"After the climb you did yesterday, the track to Col de Balme will be a walk in the park!" stated an English-speaking guide (from Texas!) much to my relief. On the ascent, I stretched out my tent to dry, while the ponies grazed the lush verges of the stony track, before continuing on to the Col. I was surprised to see crowds of people, until I noticed the chair lift which had carried them up the mountain. Many wanted to be photographed with the ponies, making me feel like the main tourist attraction! I picked out a capable-looking young man with an SLR camera, and asked if he could use mine to take some photos of us. He was with a group of Parisians who were intending to climb Mont Blanc later in the week, if the weather allowed. "You're in France now," he confirmed.

We continued along the Tour du Mont Blanc path, but the rocky surface became increasingly jagged, and I could tell by the contours on my map that the descent would be extreme. So I turned back and took the easier route down the mountain, following a track. All went well until we reached cattle grids and electric fences. To my relief, I found the fences were not switched on and therefore moveable.

I took a firm grip on the lead rope as a boy whizzed by on a bicycle. He was followed by his father, who stopped and introduced himself as John, a photographer. He suggested I camp in a car park in the small village at the bottom of the mountain, but I preferred a less public place. I found one at the base of the mountain, under some trees, although when some bikes raced past, my frightened ponies rushed towards me, as I was writing my diary. I had to move quickly too – out of the way!

Ermis stopping for a drink from a wooden water trough fed by water straight off the mountain.
Left: Heading towards Col des Poisettes.

As was my habit, I left my camp as soon as it was light enough to see, and continued down the cold, shaded valley to Argentière. Here, I bumped into the same woman from Texas who I'd met the previous day in Switzerland, followed by John the photographer, who introduced me to his wife Anne. They were working on a project to capture images of people passing through the area, so they both took photos of us. They then invited me to a breakfast of croissants at their attractive chalet, while the ponies rested in the shade of a small courtyard. Afterwards, they directed me down a pretty woodland route to Chamonix, avoiding the main road, and I parked the ponies in a hotel garden while I went to view John's photographic exhibition.

Riding through Argentière. Below:Anne Norris and her son, Luke at their chalet.

Below: Chamonix where the boulangerie proprietor gave the ponies a baguette.

36. Déjeuner à Chamonix

It was the hottest day for a week. I bought a baguette to go with my tin of tuna, and the baker gave me an extra one for the ponies, which they relished. After that, they were always trying to find bread in my saddlebags and sometimes succeeded!

Outside the bakery, I met a blonde lady and her daughter, who invited me for lunch in a grand apartment block nearby. To get the ponies into the complex, the caretaker tried to remove the garden gate from its hinges, but it wouldn't budge. Then someone suggested putting them in a neighbour's garden – they were away, and the grass needed cutting. The ponies were happy to help out.

The family were delightful and their English was much better than my French. They wined and dined me in style in their apartment, with a stunning view of the mountains, and we tucked into an array of meats and cheeses – a treat to my taste buds. As we chatted, the St. Jacques de Compostelle pilgrim trail cropped up in conversation. After lunch they offered me a shower, which was an added bonus after four days of climbing mountains.

I left at five, reluctantly, as it was still very hot. However, the ponies had finished off the neighbour's grass, and a few other plants too. I followed directions through Chamonix, and led the ponies right through the central pedestrian area. I had no idea it would take so long or be so crowded, but I just had to keep going – praying that the ponies wouldn't leave droppings in the exclusive shopping centre.

By eight in the evening, I was still uncertain where to pitch camp. We were travelling through some woodland, so I turned off the main track, up through the forest and found a grassy spot on level ground. It was secure, if noisy from the echoing roar of the river and the traffic in the valley below. I went to sleep looking at the towering mountains, but when I awoke, they were hidden by misty drizzle, so I quickly packed up before it became a downpour.

François and Anne Marie Vuarambon with Ali outside the home they built.

The problem with the traffic and river being squeezed between two mountain ranges, to the east and west, was that I needed a safer route – especially with incessant rain creating poor visibility and slippery roads. I asked at the tourist office in Les Houches, who thought the more mountainous westerly slope would be too steep and slippery. They advised me to follow the river on its east bank, where gentler forest tracks would lead to fewer 'hold your breath' moments.

When I got through the forest, during a window of dry weather, I hung my wet tent, clothes, boots and socks out on a bridge. Yoana's shoe had been clanking loudly, and I was pondering what to do next. We were all tired and feeling dampened by the rain and traffic, both in body and spirit, and I really didn't want to have to take the ponies along the main road. Just then, my phone rang.

"I wanted to meet you last night, Trace," exclaimed Ali, "but I didn't know where you would be – somewhere in the woods, but where? I have a truck which can pick you up tonight." Ali and I had been great friends for a long time, having first met in North America while teaching horse riding, and we then rode the length of New Zealand together. She now lived in France and worked with disabled people in Switzerland. We were so excited at the prospect of being reunited!

I grazed the ponies conspicuously by the main road near Luzier, and was spotted by Ali followed by one of her contacts, François, who arrived with his truck. The ponies were happy to walk in, almost as if they knew they were being spared a long walk. We were greeted at François' grand house, in the depths of Haute-Savoie, by a variety of hunting dogs of different sizes, and he proudly showed us a huge wild boar which he'd caught, now hanging in a cool room. With Ali as translator, I learnt that François had been in the army and had been the French cross country skiing champion until taking early retirement. He'd then built his own house – a typical Swiss-French mansion – and had cut, retrieved and dried all the wood himself. The framework was mostly fitted together with tongue and groove, and nails were only used in the roof, which was surfaced with slate from Cormayeur in Italy. He'd also created many ornamental woodcarvings and inserted great beams in the interior, including huge moulded timbers over the fireplaces.

"Tout avec les mains (all with my hands)," said François, smiling proudly.

110

37. Haute Savoie

For it is God who works in you to will and to act
according to his good purpose. Philippians 2v13 NIV

François offered to travel with us north to the Burgundy region, which was my original planned route back to the English Channel and home, but somehow it didn't feel right. Instead I felt a tug inside to head south.

At one point, Ali's friend Judith mentioned the Saint Jacques de Compostelle pilgrim route, one leg of which began in Geneva and continued all the way to Santiago in north west Spain. This was the fourth time I'd been told about this route. I had time to ponder this as my ponies needed a good rest, and I needed to return to my business on Dartmoor to earn money to fund the continuation of our journey across Europe – whichever direction it took us.

Ali managed to find us a large field on a steep mountain, full of long grass – probably more than my Greek ponies had ever seen in their lives! Meanwhile, I tested my improving French. While sitting in a restaurant, a waitress asked me what I would like. I confidently replied, in French, that I was waiting for two friends… but obviously didn't say that at all. Minutes later two beers arrived on the table, much to the amusement of Ali and her friend when they joined me later!

Before setting off François, helped us get packed up. He gave me a bag for my tripod and strapped it to the tent on the back of Yoana's saddle, while Ali had both sleeping bags strapped to the back of her saddle. But we didn't have the same muscle power as François to ever get it strapped together again!

After a busy period back home, focusing on my business, I returned to Geneva in mid-September.

"Did you see the snow on the mountains?" Ali asked as she collected me from the airport. "It's going to be down to 1,500 feet tomorrow."

"Oh, gosh, we had better get south quick!" I responded, for while I'd been away, I'd decided this was the way I should be going.

Ali had looked after the ponies well in my absence, feeding them grain and supplements, worming them and paying for vets to file Ermis' teeth. Although Yoana had put on a lot of weight, Ermis was still slim, despite the abundant grass and extra grain. On top of all Ali's generosity, she'd also bought me a beautiful pair of saddlebags – just the kind I'd always longed for. They were well made and had capacity for my video camera on one side and my stills camera on the other, and still left room for extra equipment. Even so, I tended to keep my stills camera looped over the cantle of the saddle, so it was at hand whenever needed.

It was cold when I was reunited with the ponies, and Ermis was shivering. Ali planned to ride with me as far as Le Puy, and we intended to leave the pack with François who would bring it to Le Puy and pick Ali up. Unfortunately, the evening before we left, our plan fell through, so Ali and I gave a frantic prayer, asking for a way to get the pack to Le Puy. Then I remembered that I had a contact near Le Puy, and one of Ali's neighbours kindly offered to look after the pack until a courier arrived. We needed to get going, as Ali was only able to take seven days off work.

As we set off on Saint Jacques de Compostelle pilgrim route, I wondered how I was going to get to Santiago before Christmas – even though we were able to trot on without the pack, and cover around 30 kilometres a day. We reached a grand, mid-19th century house in Bellegrande and asked if we could stay there. They were unsure about the ponies, but there was plenty of grass, and Ali persuaded them that they wouldn't be any trouble tethered on a tree. "Pay what you like," they said. "Welcome to the Compostelle."

Late on the second day, as we were passing through a small village, a round, cheery man with four teeth kindly showed us to the winery, but there was no spare grass to camp on, so he found us a better spot in a vineyard, although a pack of local dogs barked continuously through the night, and the following morning their very grumpy owner moaned at us in French. I watched in amazement as a small dog came flying through the air at Ermis, who nonchalantly continued to graze. When he tried to bite Yoana's hind heels, she instinctively kicked it away. The dog never returned.

Friends come and friends go,
But a true friend sticks by you like family.
Proverbs 18v24 TM

"I estimate it will take you nine weeks to get to Santiago," said Ali, as we stood beside a statue of Saint Jacques de Compostelle. "That's 30 kilometres a day, with a rest day." I was rather daunted by this. I had to be back well before Christmas to sell a stack of Dartmoor calendars and I knew very well how slowly my Greek ponies travelled – even with a plentiful supply of grain. We often covered more ground when we led them on foot.

"Maybe you'd better swap them for an Arab horse. You'd be much faster!" Ali joked.

I was shocked to read under the statue of Saint Jacque de Compostelle it was 1643 kilometres to Santiago. Somehow I was going to have to find another gear with my Greek horses! (below) Crossing the Rhône River.

113

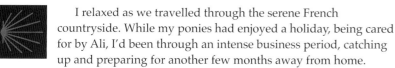 I relaxed as we travelled through the serene French countryside. While my ponies had enjoyed a holiday, being cared for by Ali, I'd been through an intense business period, catching up and preparing for another few months away from home.

The path ahead was clearly marked out by scallop shells ('concha' in Spanish) – an ancient symbol for the route to Santiago, which has guided pilgrims for centuries. The days were hot but the nights cold, as we passed through wine and apple country, before entering an area dominated by brown and white dairy cows. They lined up at the electric fences with upturned noses, curiously staring, snorting and sniffing at us as we passed. Climbing up one hill, leading Ermis behind Yoana, I noticed she had a swelling on her inside hock. She wasn't lame and I hoped it wasn't a spavin (a bony growth) caused by trotting on the roads.

We arrived at Montfaucon-en-Velay at five in the afternoon. It was still 28 degrees, even in late September. I held the ponies while Ali (who spoke fluent French) went to find accommodation. About an hour later, she returned.

"I went to the boulangerie, who sent me to the pub, who sent me to the mayor in the town hall," she said breathlessly. "I found a helpful man there. He contacted one of the guys on the council who had a field just outside town. He phoned him, and we can put our ponies in his field. I even have a key to his gîte!" We laughed together, but I did wonder how I was going to manage once Ali left me. I kept writing useful words down and practising my French, with Ali's help.

38. Montfaucon-en-Velay

In Montfaucon-en-Velay Ali found us a gite and lush field for the ponies on the edge of town.

Meeting the locals!

I was worried that Yoana's swollen hock might bring my journey to an end. Although she still wasn't lame, the swelling had grown, so we continued on foot through a volcanic area, in the direction of Le Puy, hoping to find a vet there. On one night we stayed at a campsite, and on another we slept at a chalet, but there wasn't much grazing, and the local farmers were even possessive about the roadside verges.

We crossed the River Loire over an old cobbled bridge, but at the far end we were blocked by swing gates, designed to stop vehicles and probably horses. My Greek ponies may have been slow, but they were extremely adaptable, and able to squeeze past the blockade. We continued along the river, passing apartment blocks and bridges painted with graffiti. Not a secure area to camp. Ali called our contacts in Le Puy, Monsieur and Madame Bonne, who confirmed that they'd received our pack saddle, and said there was a riding stable that we could stay at.

While Ali was on the phone, trying to contact the stables, a woman with a hunting dog stopped to speak to me. She introduced herself as Catherine, and said she was a nun. She thought we could stay at the seminary near the cathedral, but was unsure about the availability of grass. This was of utmost importance, so she offered to guide us up the hill to the riding stables.

39. Le Puy-en-Velay

We arrived unannounced at l'Espace Equestre du Velay, high up on the hill overlooking Le Puy – a town shaped by volcanic eruptions, and crowned with grand monuments including a magnificent cathedral. Although it was Sunday evening, the proprietors, Emmanuel and Anne, gave our ponies a paddock outside with hay and water, while Catherine and her dog guided us back down the hill and along narrow cobbled streets to a gite, called Le Relais du Pelerin Saint Jacques, close to the grand cathedral. Inside this 16th and 17th century building, a very hospitable hostess offered us a choice of dormitory beds. The curfew was 10 o'clock so we dashed back down the cobbled streets to find something to eat before being shut out. After walking over 30 kilometres that day, I was ready to sleep but was thankful for my earplugs, which muffled the sound of snoring in the dormitory!

The chapel of Saint Michel X1

Catherine holding Yoana while the vet dressed her hock.

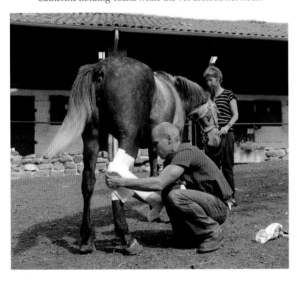

Emmanuel at the Espace Equestre riding stables asked if I wanted to swap Yoana for one of his horses. "Maybe he'll have a nice fast Arab!" suggested Ali, but despite Yoana and Ermis being so slow that other pilgrims overtook us, we knew we'd never be able to part with them!

Monsieur and Madame Bonne kindly delivered my packsaddle, and I immediately sorted through the contents to see if I could lighten the load. The time had come for Ali to head home, so we struggled down to the railway station, clutching bags of unwanted equipment, only to find that the train to Geneva was leaving within minutes.

"But you will come to meet us in Spain?" I asked, feeling forlorn that my friend had to leave so suddenly, and realising that although I had been speaking French, I'd now have to get by on my limited vocabulary. I consoled myself with the fact that at least I knew more French than Greek or Italian, and I'd coped in those countries with little more than sign language! In fact, Ali had one more job to do as translator: as she sped towards Geneva, she helped to arrange a visit to the vet, who decided that Yoana's infection was probably caused by a grass seed while she was lying down, much to my relief. We would be continuing after all.

Catherine took me sightseeing around the city, and I replaced my Italian mobile phone sim card with a French one and bought some supplies. I also found some good walking boots, as I was spending much more time on foot than anticipated.

"You have to be careful not to leave too late because of La Burle – a very strong wind which brings snow," explained Catherine. "It can make it dangerous and difficult to get to the cathedral."

I was trusting that Yoana would quickly recover thanks to the vet's daily visits. Meanwhile, the hosts at the gite directed me to the Saint Jacques information centre where a volunteer called Jean Louis helped me to upload and back up my photos.

"It is better that you go now as exercise will be good for her leg," the vet told me. I was so thankful it wasn't serious that I didn't mind paying the big bill.

Catherine decided to join me for a while, accompanied by her hunting dog, Alto, who was so strong that he pulled her along. She told me about her life as we prepared to leave Le Puy: "At 18, I went to work with horses in a man's world. I loved it so much. I was so happy," she said. "I went for one month to New Jersey in America and stayed eight years before coming back to France." She told me she'd decided not to become a 'closed order' nun because she loved her animals too much to give them up.

Walk in the ways of your heart.
Eccl. 11v9 NKJ

Le Puy-en-Velay has been one of the main departure points for the famous pilgrimage to Santiago de Compostela in north west Spain since the 10th, 11th and 12th centuries. The first pilgrim to set foot on this route was said to be Godescalc, Bishop of Le Puy, who walked to Santiago de Compostela to pay homage to St James, whose grave was apparently discovered there a century earlier. Since then, numerous others have risked the hazardous journey, following in the Bishop's footsteps, and it has grown in popularity. Today, as many as 15,000 pilgrims may gather for a blessing in LePuy before setting off on the journey. I became one of them when I bought a 'credential' at the cathedral, to identify myself as a pilgrim and to ensure cheaper accommodation en route.

Some do it because they enjoy the walk and the challenge, while others are seeking God and His direction in their lives. I was simply walking the way, which God had put in my heart. I believe that He has been directing my steps ever since I was 19, and hitch hiking through Israel to Jerusalem, when I asked Jesus into my heart.

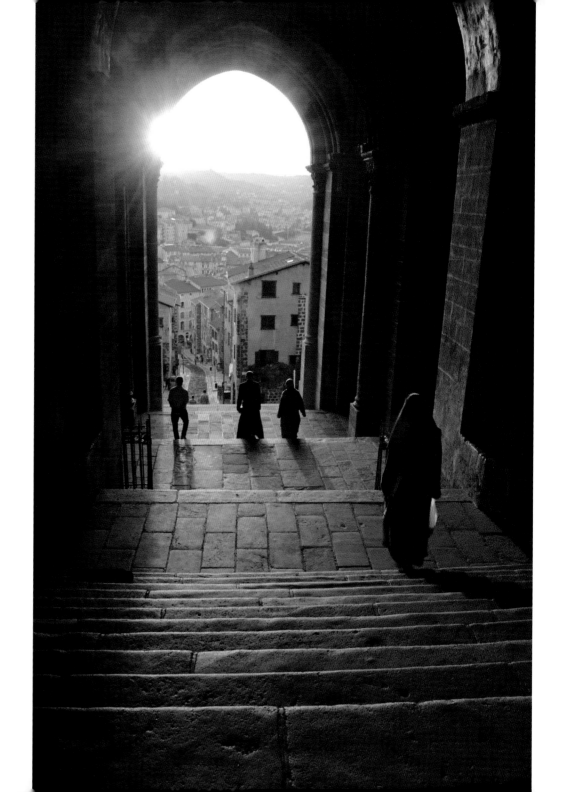

After five nights of livery, along with grain and hay, I was expecting quite a large bill. But when I asked Emmanuel and Anne how much I owed them, I had to ask again, as it was less than half the price they had initially quoted: just 70 Euros, plus extra nuts in our pack. In some places, I'd been charged that much for a single night. I was very grateful, as I had a long way to go on a limited budget – that's why I always tried to find grassy places to camp, which was tricky in France, where fences seemed to line much of the route.

Catherine collected me from the gite at five in the morning and the stable dogs sounded the alarm. It was still dark, and I was out of practice, so it took me twice as long to load the pack. Eventually we left, and wound our way through the cobbled streets before arriving at a mass that was being held for pilgrims leaving Le Puy that morning. I tied the ponies in a courtyard outside the cathedral, along with Alto, Catherine's dog (who had already escaped three times on the way there), but he howled so loudly that she had to leave the mass to calm him down.

Once the mass was over, the priest blessed all the pilgrims in front of a statue of St James and handed us all a little silver-coloured pendant, with a black Mary and Jesus and a light blue or white plastic rosary, of the sort that I would later see draped over statues and crosses along the route. In Europe, there are over 400 black Virgin Mary statues, created in medieval times, and many of these in France. Some are carved out of ebony and other dark woods, while others have become darkened by time and candle soot.

I also collected my credential form – our passport to the Camino – with its initial stamp from Le Puy cathedral itself, which would soon be joined by many other stamps from places along the route.

126

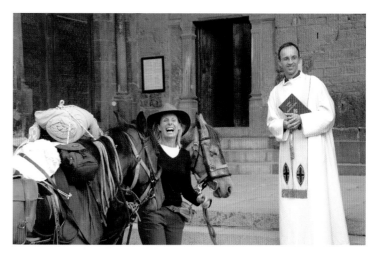

After the mass, the priest came out to bless Catherine's dog and my Greek ponies. Catherine told me when to say Amen, and Jean Louis kindly took photos. We laughed so much as I directed him, using a mixture of French, English and sign language. I was grateful that he had a good eye for photography, as he also travelled with me through the town.

Construction workers invited me for coffee but I declined as I was meeting Catherine at the square with Alto and then together following the St.Jacques de Compostele

40. Le Chemin de Saint-Jacques

Catherine and I climbed out of the valley, and looked back at the spectacular city of Le Puy, down in the valley, as we continued on tracks and roads leading to higher ground. Here, we met Gerda, a strong, tall German woman, with her Australian shepherd dog Lena, who I'd bumped into the day before in the Information Centre. She'd been walking for several months.

It was hot for late September, and Catherine was becoming exhausted, so I attached her backpack to Ermis' saddle as I was leading the ponies anyway. But then things got worse for Catherine when Alto disappeared. We hoped he may have joined some walkers who had gone on ahead of us, but when we caught up with them, they said they hadn't seen him.

Goals may give focus, but dreams give power. Dreams expand the world. – John Maxwell

Later that day, as we arrived at a beautifully converted barn at Mont Bonnet, called Grange Gite, a man arrived in small car and asked if we had lost a dog. Much to our relief, he opened the boot and out jumped Alto! He was very lame on his hind leg, so after consulting a vet, Catherine decided to take him home.

Gerda slept in my tent that night with Lena, as dogs weren't permitted in the gite. I realised that this must be a quiet time of year for the Camino, as only one table was occupied in the large dining room, with its high ceiling and wide panoramic window. I knew that in the spring and summer, thousands walked this way each month, and I'd heard there wasn't enough accommodation, especially in Spain, which was why many new 'albergues' (Spanish for hostel) were being built. It was clear that pilgrims provided a good income to businesses along the route. I had a very comfortable night here, but I missed camping out with my ponies.

41. Saint-Privat d'Allier

The ponies discovered the alfafa I had tucked into Yoana's pack!

 "You are crazy!" exclaimed a walker, as he watched me coax one pony at a time down a boulder-strewn path, criss-crossed with tree roots. At one point Ermis turned back, as he often did, just as I'd persuaded Yoana down a really difficult, steep bit. Seeing Ermis climbing back up the hill, she decided to follow him. I had to start all over again, and at first she stubbornly refused, so I asked Gerda to hold one pony while I manoeuvred the other. We got past this, only to find that the path then plunged vertically onto a road. To help keep their balance on this dangerous drop, I unsaddled them both, and prayed and encouraged them to follow me down.

"You are a tough woman!" remarked Gerda, giving me a hug. "You actually got your horses down there!"

"Phewie!" I replied, patting the ponies with relief. "Thank You God!"

Gerda kindly gave me one of her shirts, which was too big, but protected me from the sun. It was unusually warm for the autumn, and I had left my long-sleeved shirts in Geneva and to save weight – I'd only packed a couple of long-sleeved merino wool tops (which were too hot for this weather).

133

We camped just off the path – I was in my tiny tent, while Gerda slept under my tarpaulin with her dog. It was pleasantly cool the next day, and we stopped for breakfast (consisting of the usual bread and cheese) just as the milking cows were returning to grass. I gave a friendly wave to the passing farmers, as I didn't want them to resent my ponies grazing the verges, and they waved back.

Along the way, Gerda and I (and the ponies too!) enjoyed picking and eating sweet elderberries and getting juice all over our faces, like children.

At Monistrol-d'Allier we got an official stamp on our credential forms.

Do not delay, the golden moments fly! – Henry Wadsworth Longfellow

We stopped at the water fountain in Saugues, and bought coffee from waiters who laughed at my attempts to order it in French, and they weren't all that helpful when I asked where to buy grain. We found a shop, but unfortunately it was closed, so we stopped for lunch by a stream, where there was good grass for the ponies. The water was surprisingly cold, but that didn't stop Gerda stripping off and using her dog's folding water bowl as her shower. She was unabashed, and caused people crossing the bridge to look twice.

I was pretty sure the ponies fared best that night. Gerda and I were crammed into my tiny tent, along with her dog Lena, who fidgeted, snored and broke wind. I had little choice: two weeks earlier, Gerda had decided it was too cold to camp outside, so had left her tent erected beside the track with a note to say anyone could take it.

I was up and packing up at five, and we had left by six. If we'd just gone a little further the night before, we'd have reached Le Sauvage – a remote and austere structure, looking like a castle on the outside, but with several houses sheltered inside and plenty of accommodation.

Saugues at 1000 metres. Below: Le Sauvage.

Gerda said she'd have stayed there, although it wouldn't have suited me because there was no grass for the ponies. I was beginning to understand how awkward it can be to travel with others, with different needs. We stopped for a typical breakfast of bread and jam in the warm sunshine, but being so exposed I could imagine how cold it could get. Further down the road, near the chapel of St.Roche, we met a family by a fountain, who told us the water had special healing powers.

"This is the last weekend to be out in the countryside, as the snow will be coming," the man added. I didn't want to delay. It was 30 degrees in the sun, but cold in the shade, so I could imagine that the weather could change suddenly.

42. L'Aubrac

In Saint-Alban-sur-Limagnole, I phoned a place that accepted horses, but they wouldn't take dogs. They suggested a campsite, but the attendant was as sour as grass and refused to open up a caravan for Gerda. We knew that squeezing into my tent for a second night wasn't an option, so Gerda left to find accommodation in town. I'd already paid for us all (including Lena the dog), so had no choice but to stay there. I was exhausted, having not slept the previous night, and had blisters on my toes from all the walking.

I was unprepared for the cold that night, didn't sleep well and was up before dawn. The frost on my tent sparkled in the torchlight… and then my heart sank as I saw that the wire gate was down and there was no sign of the ponies – I really hoped they hadn't got out onto the main road. I continued searching the campsite until my beam of light picked them out, grazing by the caravans. I was hugely relieved, but they were disgruntled that I had no grain to offer them. "I promise I will get some today," I said, feeling bad.

I quickly saddled up and we left the frozen campsite, only to be engulfed by the mist rising off the river and surrounding marshland. We were soon reunited with Gerda and Lena, and within hours the temperature shot from freezing to 30 degrees. We passed through the undulating Aubrac region, which was attractive but parched, offering only a few isolated grassy patches to stop and graze.

At Aumont-Aubrac, we found a gite in the centre of town whose owners were only too willing to help. First, they led me to a sun-scorched paddock, and then took me to find grain. The local store only sold 50kg bags – too heavy to pack on the ponies – but we found a 25kg sack at the garden centre. Much to the ponies' delight, and my satisfaction, I gave them a generous supper to lighten the load, while I enjoyed a delicious, traditional meal of pâté, cheese, potato and sausage, cooked by the hospitable proprietors.

Unsaddling in the square at Aumont-Aubrac.

As my ponies were several kilometres from the gite, I didn't leave with all the other pilgrims and I enjoyed some solitude, although I did meet a few enthusiastic Italians. Later that morning I was reunited with Gerda and some other pilgrims, and also met some French riders who were dressed as if they were from the Wild West. They were riding through the Massif Central – an area of granite rocks which reminded me of Dartmoor, in England (albeit much drier). They were called Gerard and Claude, but I nicknamed them the French Cowboys!

The Aubrac area of the Massif Central was an area which looked similar to Dartmoor with its granite rock, albeit much drier.

Claude helped me get Yoana and Ermis through the marshy ground as they both hated to get their feet wet!

43. Nasbinals

Can two walk together, unless they are agreed? - Amos 3v3 NKJ

"You are not a pilgrim. You are just a Sunday walker," stated Gerda. "I want to travel alone in my river." I was relieved to hear this. I knew it was time to part company, and there was a heaviness about her 'spiritual river' – it lacked the joy, freedom and peace of the Holy Spirit.

Shortly afterwards we met the French cowboys again and followed them back to riding stables at Nasbinals. My friend Ali had kindly called ahead, so they were expecting us and were hospitable. The ground was devoid of grass, but at least they had some grain.

I couldn't help but fall in love with the pretty Aubrac cattle that I found here – they reminded me of Jerseys, as they were tan with white around their dark eyes and noses. The Aubrac were first bred by French monks over 150 years ago. They are hardy, with a good resistance to disease, live long and calve easily. In late spring, they are moved up to the higher ground to graze on the rich grass and flowers. Although they are mainly bred for beef, their milk is still used to make the traditional Laguiole cheese.

Gerda left the following morning, without saying goodbye, and Claude and Gerard invited me to join them as they were riding in the same direction. My ponies were much slower than their Criollo horses, which came from Argentina. Claude's horse had spent three weeks on a ship to France – the kind of long-distance transportation that fortunately doesn't happen any more – while Gerard's horse had been bred in Toulouse, in France. Although I called them the French Cowboys, Gerard was an ex-banker and Claude, who had retired from the army, also worked in finance.

The Camino path led us to a gate which was too narrow for Yoana and her pack, so Claude and Gerard kindly removed the padlocked adjacent gate from its hinges, let us through, and replaced it behind us. But they were spotted by a furious farmer, in blue overalls, who came marching down the hill towards us.

"Your horse is eating my grass!" he shouted at Claude, even though there wasn't much grass to eat, we were on a public path and we weren't stopping on his land. He escorted us up and across his property, which was shrouded in mist. It slowly evaporated to reveal extensive, undulating fields.

A merry heart does good like medicine.
Proverbs 17v22 NKJ

I enjoyed the company of the French Cowboys, and we laughed as we tried to communicate, although Claude's English was much better than my French.

"You are a very unusual woman," said Gerard. "Crocodile Dundee woman!"

Ermis and Yoana moved faster in the company of the Criollo horses and we easily covered 30 kilometres, although Yoana, with her mare-ish attitude, was bossy towards them. Ermis, in his quiet way, was much the smallest but was still in charge.

"Women have given me trouble all my life!" said Gerard, worried that Yoana might kick their geldings. He then pointed to some snake holes: "Attention! I had a horse bitten," he warned me, gesturing with two fingers under his throat.

On the descent to Saint-Côme-d'Olt, we met an 80-year-old farmer.

"Maybe he went to school with my mother?" Claude remarked. "My family come from here, and they are the same age!"

44. Couvent de Malet

You chart the path ahead of me
and tell me where to stop and rest.
Psalm 139v3 NLT

"Do you have a reservation?" Gerard teased as we arrived at the magnificent old Couvent de Malet.

"No, but it looks like there are lots of rooms," I said, gazing up at the stone building, glowing in the evening sun.

Our hostess, Anne Marie, was so hospitable and suggested putting the ponies in a large chicken enclosure, which did have edible vegetation, including some grass, old fruit trees and a rose bush (which I knew wouldn't be there in the morning!).

The ponies were waiting at the chicken gate early the next day, eager for their breakfast of grain. I was getting packed up when Claude suggested I ask Anne Marie if there was a place with more grass for the ponies. She was very obliging and showed me to a big, grassy field, which sealed my decision: this was going to be a rest day.

My cowboy friends asked me to lunch in St Côme, as this was their final destination, and Claude reminisced about his childhood, when he used to visit his grandparents here.

"This is a gastronomic area," Gerard told me, as we sat outside a restaurant in the sunny square.

"I thought all France liked their food?"

"Yes, but this area is especially good!"

I was sad to say goodbye to my fun French Cowboys.

"Crocodile Dundee woman, you need one of these for your journeys!" stated Gerard, pointing to their Criollo horses as they were loaded into a trailer. "They are good endurance horses."

That evening I met a young Frenchman who had taken 75 days to walk the Camino all the way from Le Puy to Santiago in Spain.

"Take spray for the bedbugs in the Spanish albergues (hostels)," he warned me. "And you'd better hurry up, as it dropped to minus seven on the high desert plains this time last year."

Dreams come through much business and painful effort. Eccl. 5v3 AMP

I was trying to download and back up my photos onto a PC, but I was getting frustrated, partly because I use an Apple Mac, and partly because this computer only spoke French.

Just then, a pilgrim called Monique remarked: "Your life is like a fairy tale!"... which certainly didn't feel true at that particular moment.

"I really hadn't thought of my life like that before," I replied, and her comment got me thinking. Yes, I was blessed, as I was doing what I really loved – travelling with horses and taking photographs – but it had taken years to build up my business, and to gain this freedom. Also, I still had dreams to fulfil which would take faith and hard work.

Monique kindly translated some signs around St Côme, including some very graphic diagrams on a church wall, showing how medicines were taken in medieval times. This had been a wine-growing area in the 19th century but a disease killed off a lot of the vines. Many local people emigrated to southern Brazil, while protestants from south east France, who were persecuted by the Catholics, headed for Argentina.

The ponies were enjoying the plentiful grass but I couldn't get hold of any more grain. I was concerned about Ermis whose ribs were still showing, even after Ali had wormed him and had his teeth filed.

"Trace, you must get to Spain before the weather turns bad," Ali told me over the phone, in a concerned tone, before arranging a lift for us all to St Jean Pied De Port, near the Spanish border.

45. St. Jean Pied de Port

"You are crazy!" remarked Angelique, who ran some stables in the Basque region of the Pyrenees – an area which reminded me of Wales. "I tried two days on the camino – it was too hard going, so I came home!"

That night, ominous dark clouds rolled over the surrounding mountains and I wondered which route I should take. One option was the traditional Camino Francés, which climbed up and over the Pyrenees and across the high plains, but the grass would be sparse here at this time of year, and the coming rain could turn to snow any day soon. The other option was the Camino del Norte, which followed the northern coast. There would be more grass on this route, as it was much wetter, but it was longer with more stressful traffic, which I had experienced enough of in Greece and Italy, preferring the quieter routes, although the Camino Francés would still take us through some very large cities.

Angelique took me in her car to show me a shortcut to St Jean Pied De Port, but we both got totally confused in the twisting lanes. On the way, we met a Frenchman on a grey pony, with a large dog, who was travelling to the Camino del Norte. Angelique asked if I wanted to join this man, but I declined (I later heard he'd been turned back at the Spanish border). Instead, I decided to take the longer route to the town – I didn't want to get lost before I even started my ascent over the Pyrenees.

On the outskirts, I tied the ponies outside a supermarket while I bought some supplies. When I came out, I found that Ermis has untied himself and was about to wander onto the road. I quickly put my shopping down, but he picked up the litre of milk in his teeth and burst the carton, which spurted all over us. To avoid wasting any more, I drank the rest on the spot.

It was lunchtime when I arrived in town and the information centre was closed, but the people were friendly and pointed me in the direction of the Route de Napoléon – so called because it was used by the French general to move his troops to and from Spain during the Peninsular War. It was also favoured by the pilgrims in the Middle Ages, to avoid being robbed by bandits hiding in the woods which lined an alternative path near the coast (there were still thieves along the Camino today!). For this section of the route, I had a gem of a guide book, written in English by John Brierley, called 'Camino de Santiago', which was packed with interesting tips. Near the front I found these words by William Arthur Ward:

But risks must be taken because the greatest hazard in life is to risk nothing.

The person who risks nothing, does nothing, has nothing, is nothing.

He may avoid suffering and sorrow,

But he cannot learn, feel, change, grow or live.

Chained by his servitude he is a slave who has forfeited all freedom.

Only a person who risks is free.

Following directions from some friendly market girls, and with my guidebook close to hand, I began my ascent of the Pyrenees. It was a bright, sunny day, which I appreciated because the previous day had been cold and wet. I'd been told that this route would be crowded with pilgrims but it was surprisingly quiet, so I enjoyed the sun and solitude as I led the ponies up the mountain. I was expecting it to be a challenging climb, and wondered if I really was following the 'difficult' route I had heard about – it was so much easier than the Mont Blanc trail.

I spotted a girl approaching from a distance, her sturdy walker's legs backlit by the sun.

"This is the best part – on the other side it's dry and brown," she told me. "So I returned to this section of the Camino. I want to come and live here!" I agreed it was a stunning area, and after hearing what she'd said, I took my time and enjoyed the amazing scenery. I also had an uneasy feeling that grass for the ponies was going to be scarce on the high, dry plains ahead.

"I'm getting splashed!" exclaimed a woman outside the Albergue d'Orisson, as I tried to fill my bag with water, while being barged by the ponies who were desperate for a drink. I wondered whether she was also attempting the Camino. I knew it was going to be a test of endurance and suspected she might need to toughen up a bit.

"I didn't go fast, but I kept going," remarked Pierre from Belgium, who I met before we left. He had been walking for five weeks.

"Bon courage!" a farmer called out, as he herded some cattle down the mountain. I climbed on and up, past vast stretches of open land grazed by flocks of Manech sheep, whose high quality milk is used for the famous Ossau Iraty cheese. Curious ponies approached us, wearing coloured fabric collars, and cavorted in a circle around us. They looked like Scottish Highland ponies, and I wondered if they might be Basque mountain horses. Or maybe they were the endangered Pottok breed, native to the Basque region of France and Spain, and believed to be represented in ancient cave paintings.

I have spread my dreams beneath your feet. Tread softly because you tread on my dreams. - W.B Yeats

The human spirit once stretched by an adventure of faith will never return to its original size. - Unknown

46. The Pyrenees

The soft evening light and the elongated shadows were captivating, and I had to drag myself away from photographing sheep against the Pyrenees. We were above the tree line and I was conscious that the sun would suddenly disappear – I urgently needed to find a sheltered place to camp. We hurriedly climbed over Col de Bentartea, and descended into Spain, passing down an alley of beech trees. Here, the path levelled out enough to pitch a tent, so I tethered the ponies to the stunted tree branches. Judging by the cropped grass, it was clearly a popular shelter for sheep and mountain ponies too, so I gave Ermis and Yoana more grain. I awoke at five the next morning, but it wasn't light enough to pack up until eight. I retraced our steps back to the highest point, just to have one last, long look back into France. The air was fresh and I could hear the chimes of the sheep bells, and see the griffon vultures, with their massive wingspan (up to 2.5m, or 8ft across), soaring over the mountains – home to the largest concentration of griffons in the world.

    To capture this special moment, I set the tripod up and ran back and forth… until Ermis got fed up looking at the view. He took off down the mountain back into France, but fortunately had second thoughts and waited until Yoana and I caught up with him!

SPAIN ~ ESPAÑA

47. Navarra

It was a sparkling October day, and the cold nights had caused the edges of the beech leaves to turn yellow and orange. We lingered at Col de Lepoeder (1,450 metres), gazing at the far-reaching views westward into the mountainous Navarre region – home to a largely independent Basque community. The path was so steep that I took a more gentle option, following a small road. Here, I found good grass for the ponies, who grazed while I gazed down at the village of Roncesvalles, tucked away in the tree-cloaked valley – one of the largest surviving beech forests in Europe. It reminded me that I'd soon need to speak Spanish. I'd done an intensive six-week course, but that was ten years ago! I also read my guide book, which told me that Roncesvalles was the main entry point for Spanish pilgrims walking to Santiago, and ever since the 12th century its hospital had accepted travellers of all faiths. Today, I read, walking the Camino is even offered as an alternative to prison for some offenders.

We arrived at the valley floor and passed a towering Gothic building which was the main 'albergue' (hostel) for pilgrims, containing more than 120 beds in a single dormitory.

"Can you imagine? Trying to sleep in a room with 100 people snoring!" I exclaimed, as we moved quickly on, making the most of the comfortably warm weather – so much better than the heat of Greece and central Italy.

790 Kilometres from Roncesvalles to Santiago!
Meeting the Korean boys again on the bridge.

A feast of alfafa growing like weed on the side of the main road.

The Greeks have given us one of he most beautiful words of our language, the word "enthusiasm" – a God within. - Louis Pasteur

There were still several more hours of daylight, so we continued through a huge forest. A sign informed us that it was the haunt of witches in the 16th century, and nine people were burnt at the stake. Beside it stood a white cross – a symbol of divine protection for all who entered. After finding our way past a narrow gate, the track became a paved pathway, much to my dismay. It was slippery for the ponies, with fencing on either side and no grass to camp on. As we struggled on, an energetic group of young Koreans, who I'd passed while they were playing music on the Col de Lepoeder, now overtook us carrying their guitar.

It was twilight when I spotted a grassy track, and we dived down it. I thought my hiding place had been discovered twice – once when a car's headlights illuminated us and later when I saw the moonlit silhouette of a man on the track. I usually prefer lighter coloured horses for photographs, but I was glad these two were darker, as they were better camouflaged.

I was up at five and we'd left by six, but it was so dark in the woods, even with my torch, that I took a wrong turn and we had to retrace our steps. As we passed through a village, I was very conscious of the ponies' hooves echoing loudly through the streets. It reminded me of a sign I'd seen in France asking pilgrims not to used their walking sticks in the early mornings, to avoid waking people up.

We walked on through an autumn-coloured beech forest, reached the Arga River and crossed over a bridge called Puente de la Rabia (there was a legend that any animal led three times around its central arch would be cured of rabies!). On the other side, I was reunited with the Koreans and met a couple of Australians at a tourist office. I also learnt some essential Spanish words, including one for 'hay'… although I later discovered, after being given straw several times, that they'd given me the wrong word!

"I expect we'll see you in Pamplona," said Tony, who worked at the Australian consulate in Madrid.

The further west we travelled, the dryer the land became. I was getting concerned – would I be able to get enough grain or should we divert to the coast? I spied an overgrown path off the main Camino, and followed it to a peaceful camping spot with plenty of rough grass, away from traffic and buildings.

The following morning, I braced myself as we drew near to the city of Pamplona. As we followed the walkway beside the river, I called out "buenos dias!" to everyone I met, until there were just too many to greet. Many wore expressionless masks, which sometimes creased into a surprised smile or a raised eyebrow, accompanied by an occasional grunt, but most people ignored us. But then I came to the complete contrast: a playground of children, who rattled the fence in their excitement. I waved back, wishing I could remember enough Spanish to tell them our story. I mused at the sad contrast between the young, enthusiastic children and the expressionless adults, who seemed like the walking dead.

48. Pamplona

It was very cheering to be welcomed into Pamplona by Tony, the friendly Australian, and to be able to converse in the same language. He guided me over the drawbridge and through the main plaza of the old city to the tourist information centre, where he held the ponies as they grazed on a small patch of grass. I popped inside to ask where I could leave the ponies overnight, so that I could explore the city, but there were no riding stables and nowhere to buy grain – the nearest place was 19km away and not even on my route. When I got back to the ponies, Tony was being told off by a local man.

"This is a very clean city. It's not the Camino," he was saying – even though the ponies had done nothing wrong!

Tony kindly looked after them in a parched park, surrounded by fortifications, while I raced around to get my phone set up for Spain, and bought another memory card and USB sticks for my photos. Then we settled down for a picnic. Tony, being Australian, felt the cold so he sat in the sun, but I found it too hot, so I sat in the shade. At 4pm, I realised I needed to quickly make my way out of the huge city and find somewhere to spend the night. As Tony escorted me along the route, lined with conch shells to indicate that it was the Camino, a policeman stopped us and pointed to the droppings which one of the ponies had left on the pavement.

"Okay Tony, I know you're from the Australian embassy, but I'm going to need your help with Spanish here!" I said, as I handed him the reins and went back to scrape the dung into the gutter with my foot.

"Since you arrived in this city you've upset three people!" he commented with a smile, on my return.

"But what about all the people who stopped and enjoyed watching the ponies pass by?" I responded. I pictured the days when horses were a rich man's form of transport, and Pamplona must have been filled with knights in armour, clattering over the cobbles.

"I bet they didn't complain when the legendary Spanish knight, El Cid, rode his horse through their streets!"

Charlemagne's army damaged the walls of Pamplona despite them promising they would not harm the city and so the Basques retaliated by massacring the rearguard of his army at Roncesvalles.

As there were no nearby stables to keep the ponies securely overnight, I didn't have the opportunity to look around Pamplona, which was disappointing. This historic city is well known for the 'Running of the Bulls', held during the seven-day festival of Sanfermines in July – similar events are also held in towns and villages in Spain, Portugal, Southern France and even in Mexico and Nevada. Anyone over the age of 18 can take part, dressed in white shirts, red waistbands and red neckerchiefs. After singing a benediction, they run through the streets, chased by the bulls, and head for the bullring. The American writer Ernest Hemingway first brought this to international attention, and now thousands flock to the area to witness the spectacle. It's incredibly dangerous – Tony knew an Australian who had been seriously injured – and during the past 100 years, 16 people have been killed.

The sun was sinking fast when I reached the far side of Pamplona. I stopped to water the ponies and fill up my water bottles before continuing into the dusk, through a barren expanse of harvested wheatfields fringed with sparse trees. I was looking intently for a hidden place to camp, as we were still uncomfortably close to the suburbs and not far from the ugly tower blocks which seem to occupy the outskirts of many cities. I tried to enter one small copse, but the undergrowth was too rough and dense. I hurriedly moved on down cracked, dried tracks, but they were scattered with litter which meant that uncaring people lived here, so I didn't stop. I then followed a hedge until I found a short row of trees beside a hard-earthed, harvested wheatfield – I hoped they would give us some camouflage… until a huge moon rose and illuminated the landscape. The ponies picked hungrily at the bushes and the straw stubble, and I regretted being unable to buy them food in Pamplona.

The ground was too hard for my tent pegs, which buckled when I tried to get them into the ground by stepping on them. I was worried that the tent could collapse and that the ponies didn't have enough to eat. I prayed that I'd soon find grain, that we wouldn't blow away, and that no one would find us that night.

It was cool the following morning. I was up before six to pack up and was ready to head out into the parched landscape at daybreak. As I left, leading the ponies, we turned the corner and saw a man wandering in the direction of our campsite.

"Thanks God – good timing!" I sighed, as I hadn't wanted anyone to find us.

The first wave of determined, marching pilgrims passed me as I was photographing the early light spreading across the dry, stubbled fields. A little while later I came across a large pool of water, surrounded by grass – an oasis in the parched landscape – and I regretted not pushing on to discover it the previous night.

Some pilgrims hailed me: "We've been following your ponies' droppings for several days! We wondered if we'd catch up with you," said an Irishman, who was travelling with his son and two Dutchmen.

Ermis, Yoana and I joined the cast iron sculpture of pilgrims on the summit of the Sierra del Perdón.

It was a long climb up the Alto del Perdón (Hill of Forgiveness), past huge wind turbines and a dramatic sculpture representing a line of pilgrims.

My heart sank as I looked westwards – all I could see was a sun-dried, ochre expanse, interspersed with dark green trees.

"Where am I going to find enough grass for the ponies?" I asked myself with concern.

It was windy and cool here on the high ground, and we stumbled over the stony track, whose baked pebbles seemed to radiate heat. I really felt for my ponies who hungrily grabbed at the long, dry blades of grass which edged the track.

By mid-afternoon it was hotter still, and I could only imagine how intense it must be in the middle of summer – maybe as hot as Greece had been. We entered a quiet village at siesta time and there before our eyes, like a mirage, was an irrigated village green, covered in bright green clover, with a tap for drinking water. It was soothing to our eyes and to my ponies' stomachs!

While my ponies grazed, I met a trail of international pilgrims who stopped to fill their water bottles. There were people from Hungary, Brazil and South Africa, and a German man whose blisters were so bad that he was attempting to walk barefoot.

"Others have gone before without shoes!" he informed us. "It should only take a few weeks for my feet to harden up." Later that afternoon, after a good graze, we passed him tottering along the path. I admired him for his endurance.

49. Puente La Reina

When we got to Puente La Reina, I phoned the owner of the local stables. Although neither of us could understand much of the conversation, I did work out that it would cost €25 per pony per night, but at least they could have grain and hay. But when I got there, I found that he only had oats, and no hay. The owner insisted this was enough, but I knew my ponies needed much more, and that finding a food store at that time of day would be impossible – we might as well have spent the night out in the countryside. As I couldn't camp with the ponies, he took me to a campsite where I met up with the Irish and Dutch pilgrims again, and their company cheered me up.

In the morning, I bought 45kg of grain from the stables at a highly inflated price. I attached 15kg to Yoana and strapped the other 30kg sack to Ermis' saddle using bungees, which were already stretched, and I was worried they wouldn't hold. However, the salesman assured me in Spanish that it would be okay and was in a hurry for me to depart, so he escorted me out of the gate.

The ponies grabbed at blades of grass beneath the hedges as I left – I wasn't happy that they were leaving the livery stables feeling hungry. It wasn't long before the grain strapped to Ermis' saddle began to shift, and I had to use my shoulder to shove it back into place. Then, as we were crossing over a bridge, it fell off altogether. A man helped me to lift it back onto the saddle, and some friendly Irish women, who walked the Camino for two weeks each year, kindly stopped to take some photos of us.

Puente La Reina, the beautiful Romanesque Queens bridge was built for the safe crossing of the increasing number of medieval pilgrims who walked the Camino.

50. Estella

Throughout the day, I had to continually adjust the moving sack of grain. Eventually, the constant friction caused the sack to rip open and oats poured onto the ground, much to the ponies' delight and my despair.

"Okay, now you've had breakfast, lunch and afternoon tea!" I told them, wondering how I was ever going to carry the necessary grain all the way across northern Spain. I was using my bedroll cover to scoop it off the ground when an American cyclist stopped and kindly gave me a hand to lift the heavy oats back into Ermis' saddle. Entering Estella, I waved down a man in a pick-up, towing a trailer, and used my basic Spanish to ask him if he knew of any stables nearby. He made a call and marked a location on my map.

Ermis and Yoana enjoying an extra feed when the bag split.

Estella was bigger than I'd anticipated, so I pressed on to get clear of the buildings before dark, asking people if they knew the way to the stables. I followed their vague waves until I spotted the man I'd met earlier, kindly waiting for me at a junction. The people there were helpful, gave the ponies oats and hay for a very good price, and offered me a stable to sleep in (but warned me not to open the yard gate because of the dangerous guard dogs!). As I was concerned about getting enough food for the ponies I asked them if I should divert to the coastal route, where there would be more grass.

"It will take much longer as you have to go inland, to avoid the many estuaries," I was told. "This route is the most direct, but you have to hurry – bad weather is coming."

I went to sleep that night calculating how much food I'd need and when, based on the fact that we covered 20 to 30 kilometres a day, during which time each pony would eat five kilos. Even so, I couldn't be sure that I'd find any oats when I needed it, as riding stables seemed to be few and far between. There was little vegetation, so each time the ponies spied a tuft of alfafa growing at the sides of the path, or even further afield, they'd make a dive for it and drag me with them. Yoana amazed me – she was such a good 'doer' and although the larger of the two, she still looked very healthy. Ermis, on the other hand, had been thin from the very beginning and I was concerned for him. Yoana now carried the pack, Ermis carried the grain on the saddle, and I had to walk. I had good boots, but my feet swelled, causing blisters on my toes.

Children thrilled that they could lead the ponies through the village.
The owner of the stables securing the sack on Ermis' saddle.

The following morning, the owner kindly gave me a second sack for the grain and secured it to Ermis' saddle. The ponies now knew where it was, so I had to prevent them ripping the sack open with their teeth as we travelled!

We visited the ancient Monasterio Irache where the Bodega (local winery) offered pilgrims free wine, from a drinking fountain. I tied the ponies to a tree while I went to see this, and also visited the wine museum. The attendant chatted to me in Spanish, asked if I was single, told me he was and gave me a small bottle of wine! I politely thanked him and hurriedly left before the conversation got too complicated for my basic Spanish.

51. The Milky Way

You stretch out the starry curtain of the heavens. Psalm 104v2 NLT

"I've heard of you," said Chantal, a Canadian, who introduced herself as I was trying to get a photo between two arches at the Fuente de los Moros – a 13th century fountain. Every time I positioned the ponies and rushed down the steps to take the picture, they would move, so Chantal offered to help. We walked for a while together and were reunited later that evening at Los Arcos.

"You are limping!" she remarked, after I'd completed another 30 kilometre day. She and another Spanish walker, called José, asked in the town if there was overnight accommodation for the ponies. There was none, so I continued on through Los Arcos and out into the dry plains, where the farmers were harrowing the rock hard, ploughed earth, creating a dusty haze in the evening light. Although my feet were sore, I loved travelling through these atmospheric, quiet evenings.

As the light faded, I prayed for a good place to camp. Just before dark, I saw some trees and led the ponies across a ploughed stretch of ground to find a hidden area, covered in tall, dry grass. I quickly unpacked the ponies, poured some grain onto plastic bags so that none would be wasted and ate my bread, cheese and wine (courtesy of the Bodegas) in the dark. After saying goodnight to the ponies, I lay on my sleeping roll, contentedly listening to the sound of my ponies munching while gazing up at the multiplying stars.

El Camino de Santiago is a Spanish name for the Milky Way, as in the Medieval Ages the Milky Way was thought to have been formed by the dust raised by the travelling pilgrims.

I awoke before dawn with a cold head, but warmed up by feeding and then packing and saddling the ponies. We left our great campsite quickly, as the farmers had already begun harrowing. The rising sun transformed the dusty, brown scenery into a glowing pink.

Most of the riverbeds were as dry and stony as the landscape, but sometimes my ponies found a patch of grass, usually alfafa, bravely lingering there. As we travelled through this arable land, with no sign of animals, I worried about where we'd find the next grain store.

173

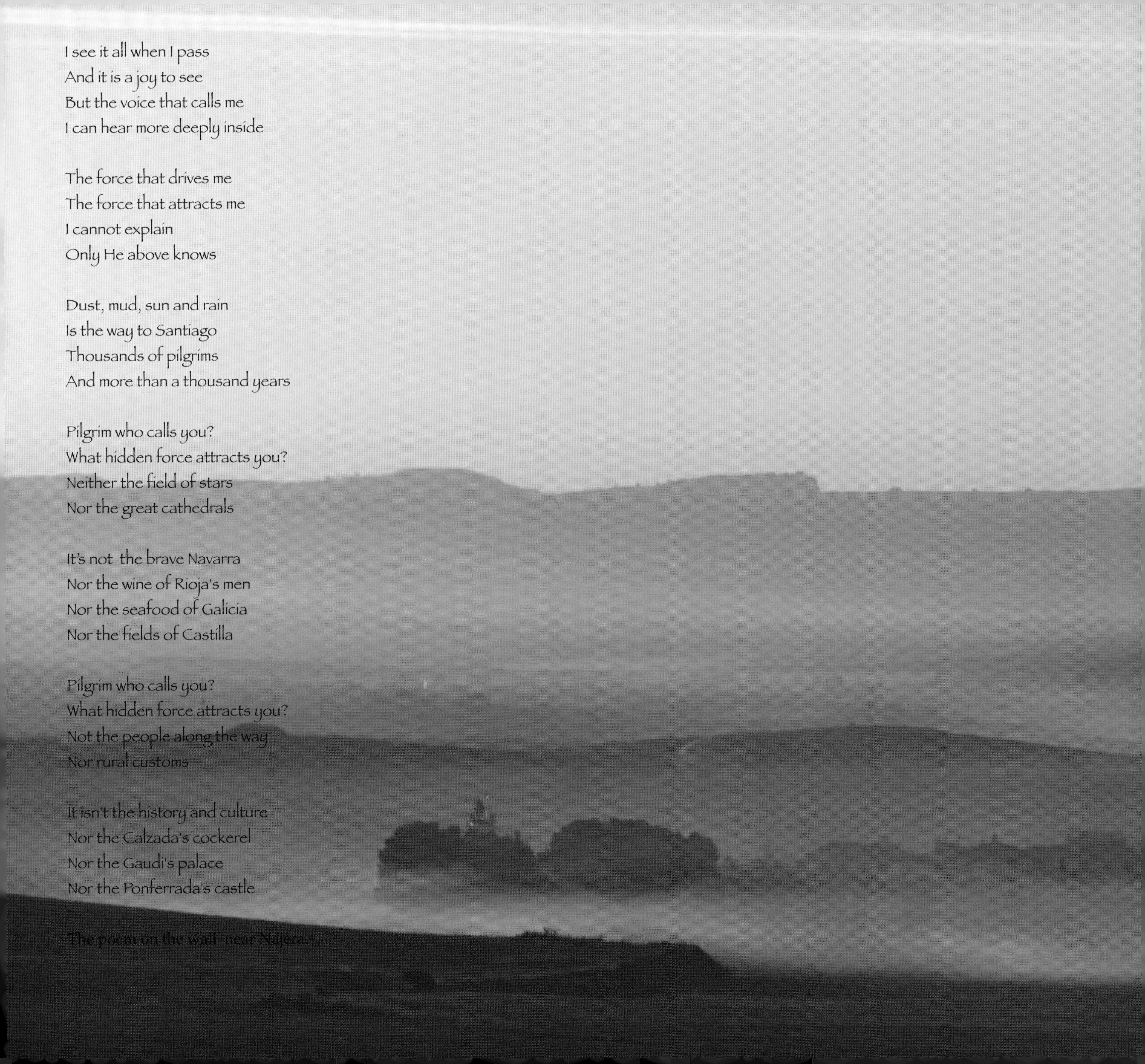

I see it all when I pass
And it is a joy to see
But the voice that calls me
I can hear more deeply inside

The force that drives me
The force that attracts me
I cannot explain
Only He above knows

Dust, mud, sun and rain
Is the way to Santiago
Thousands of pilgrims
And more than a thousand years

Pilgrim who calls you?
What hidden force attracts you?
Neither the field of stars
Nor the great cathedrals

It's not the brave Navarra
Nor the wine of Rioja's men
Nor the seafood of Galicia
Nor the fields of Castilla

Pilgrim who calls you?
What hidden force attracts you?
Not the people along the way
Nor rural customs

It isn't the history and culture
Nor the Calzada's cockerel
Nor the Gaudi's palace
Nor the Ponferrada's castle

The poem on the wall near Nájera.

Compostela means " field of dreams."

52. La Rioja - Logroño

The sound of our hooves echoed through the old, shady streets of Viana, a major pilgrim site since the 15th century. I noticed the remains of numerous pilgrim hospitals and concluded that due to the exertion, poor weather, bad diet and little money, many must have fallen ill. In fact, I'd seen several memorials to modern day pilgrims who had died on the walk.

We left the fortified city down a steep ramp, and Ermis' hooves began to slip, as if it was made of ice. My heart was thumping – Yoana was following, and I dreaded them both slipping over. Ermis instinctively reversed back up the slope and, with relief, we found another exit. We took a lunch break near a fountain, but I was disappointed to find nothing for the ponies to eat – just rubbish and human waste.

"Tracey! I'm so glad you're here." I was surprised to hear my name, and to see Chantal with my bucket! "You left it by the fountain. We were going to ask a passing cyclist to take it to you." I was so grateful – the bucket was vital for the ponies, as the only available water on the Camino came from taps.

We arrived late in the afternoon at the huge city of Logroño. There were two narrow lanes of traffic on the main bridge, and the pavement was crowded with pedestrians. There wasn't room for both ponies and they caused a traffic jam, until a girl in high heeled shoes came to my rescue. She led Ermis along the pavement, while I followed with Yoana.

The paved streets were as slippery as ice for the ponies, so I tried to make a detour while keeping as close to the edge as possible. Just then, a smartly dressed old lady staggered towards us, clutching at the walls. She looked drunk, but I was concerned she could be having a heart attack and couldn't get past us. "Ayuda! (help!)," I called, and a young man caught the old lady just before she fell into the ponies and helped her over to some other people across the street. I moved on, knowing she was in safe hands, eager to get off the slippery surface.

I was happy to bump into Chantal and José again, and they held my ponies while I dashed into the tourist information office, where I was told the only stables were 10 kilometres outside the city. It was already 6pm, so I wasn't going to make it before dark, but I knew I had to get the ponies out of the city.

"The Camino goes that way," said Chantal, pointing up the busy main street, past a large water fountain. I headed off slowly, as Ermis was dragging on the lead, and we were soon blocking a traffic lane. I tried riding him and leading Yoana instead, which at least made me more visible to the heavy traffic, but then my heart sank as we reached a barrier – the main street was sectioned off and all traffic diverted. I knew I was going to get lost.

Then a lady asked "Camino?", and pointed me in the right direction. She later caught up with me, escorted me to her apartment block, invited me to stay and suggested I leave the ponies on a small patch of grass. I thanked her, but I couldn't explain in Spanish why it wasn't a good idea to leave my ponies overnight in a city of 130,000 people, as they could be stolen.

I was racing the light to find a secure place to camp, and travelled through a park, against a flow of walkers, runners and roller skaters, hoping we wouldn't collide. There was no grass to be found… but then I was delighted to see a patch of long grass behind a post and rails. Through the gloom, I could hear quacking in the water, and guessed it must be a wildlife reserve. Once I'd unsaddled the ponies, I squeezed them through a narrow gap, relying on the darkness to hide us from passers-by, and camped beside a hide for bird watchers.

I could hear people chatting in a nearby café, and my sleep was also interrupted by shots – some kind of deterrent to predators, perhaps – but we left at dawn without being spotted, and the ponies were satisfied, with full stomachs. As I exited the park I passed a 'no camping' sign, but by then it was too late. I made one cyclist angry as the ponies blocked a narrow section of path, but another gave me a bunch of delicious grapes – a sign that we were now in the famous La Rioja wine region.

Never give up! Never give up! Never, never, never give up! ~ Winston Churchill

The Rioja country, with its vine-clad hills, was hot even in October. I bought a €1 bottle of local wine and enjoyed sipping it from my tin cup, with bread and cheese, at my various camp spots. I was glad to be following the Camino in the autumn when there were fewer pilgrims – it also meant I'd be reunited with the same people time and again, especially if we covered the same distance every day. One morning, after camping on the brow of a hill amongst pine trees, I was clip clopping through a small town and met a crowd of familiar faces from South Africa and Hungary, along with Chantal and José.

At Santo Domingo De Calzada, I was directed all over the place in my quest for 'avena' (oats), and trudged up and down the streets in the heat. I eventually asked at a John Deere tractor dealership, thinking they might speak English, but they didn't and sent me back to where I'd come from. Eventually I found a warehouse, where a man who kept saying, "Trigo, no (wheat, no!)", and rubbed his stomach as a sign that the ponies would get colic, before adding: "cebada, avena, si!" (barley, oats, yes!). All he had to sell me was barley, but without oats I knew this would cause the ponies to overheat. He wrote "5% avena" on the sack, and indicated that I should mix it, but didn't know where I could buy oats. As a result, Yoana was carrying too much barley, which was useless on its own.

At a stream, I mixed some of my remaining oats with barley for the ponies and washed my hair and socks. A Portuguese couple stopped and asked me how I was able to do all of this on my own, and I told them that it was down to my faith in God. They understood, and we walked together to Nájera. On the way, they translated a poem written on a wall, entitled 'Pilgrim who calls you?'.

We stopped by a statue of Saint James, but I was told to move the ponies off the grass, so I found another patch on the outskirts, watered by an overflow from a garage. While they grazed, the wind began to increase and the sky darkened. By the time we left, it had begun to rain and I struggled in the gale to secure the tarpaulin over the pack.

This was the first storm I had experienced, and it was wild. The rain made the soil so sticky that it stuck to our feet, and we were exhausted when we arrived at Grañón. The local priest let me graze the ponies in front of a convent for 20 minutes, while I charged my phone, and then suggested I put the ponies in a nearby playing field which was brown and bare. They also offered me my first shower for a week and a light supper while the ponies ate my last oats mixed with barley. I was concerned that they had no hay, so a Spanish pilgrim called José asked around town and found some dusty straw in a lady's attic, which the ponies didn't want to touch! We were cold, the ponies were hungry, my back ached and I considered giving up.

(For English translation of poem see page 174)

When I pray you answer me; you encourage me by giving me the strength I need. Psalm 138v3 NLT

Even in this bare, dry land, Ermis always loved to roll at every opportunity. I assume that until I'd bought him, he'd been kept in a place where rolling was impossible, as I had never seen such a dull, matted coat on a horse. His ribs had always shown through, and they still did, although at least he now had a shiny coat. He loved a good brush, as did Yoana, who would wiggle her top lip with delight.

179

I met local people and walked with pilgrims from all over the world including a shepherd, David from north Devon, a Frenchman and Norbert Szekeres from Hungary who took the above photograph.

The following morning my back ached from lifting heavy grain, so I left seven kilos of barley at the convent, for the next traveller with animals. We headed off into the brown landscape, but made slow progress that day, as we kept stopping to graze the edges of the track – wherever there was a remnant of grass and alfafa.

It was a treat to find a grassy place to camp that night, with water and hidden from sight (but not from the noise of a busy road). After dark, we were visited by some cows and I shooed them away – concerned that they might take fright and trample over my tent. The following morning, it was very cold, and the ground was white with frost.

While I was packing up, a figure appeared out of the darkness. It turned out to be a man called David, who I'd met previously and who had walked all the way from north Devon in England, carrying a didgeridoo. We travelled together as far as Atapuerca – a famous little village where archaeologists found the earliest human remains in Europe. I stopped here to allow the ponies to graze on a grassy verge, intending to catch up with David later.

A Spanish couple offered me a marrow. They asked me if I was wealthy and I tried to explain in Spanish that I was not and had to camp most of the way. They warned me to be careful.

Before leaving the village, I filled up my water bottles on the village green while the ponies grazed some more, but was asked to move on. However, we were directed to the grassiest place I had seen in all my time in Spain! It was like an oasis – a lush, green patch of grass with a pond and two channels of running water, shaded by willow trees. I lay on my side, knowing that my back strain would prevent me from getting up if I lay flat, and stayed there for several hours, listening to the birds chattering in the willows. I was so exhausted, but had to avoid falling asleep just to keep an eye on the ponies, in case they rolled with their packs and saddles. It was such a lovely place that I was tempted to stay, but doubted I'd be allowed to, so close to the centre of the village.

53. Atapuerca

Yoana kneeling down to drink from the water chanel - a clever mare!

He lets me rest in green meadows; he leads me beside peaceful streams.
He renews my strength. Psalm 23v3 NLT

As I was leaving, an older man asked me, in Spanish, where I was going. I shrugged my shoulders and pointed over the hill. I thought I'd misunderstood his reply, but he seemed to be inviting me to stay in the oasis. His son, Santiago, spoke English and confirmed that this was indeed what he'd offered. And to make me even happier, they knew a man who grew oats and took me to buy some!

My silent prayer had been answered. The father suggested I pitch my tent under the willows to avoid the dew, and so I rested in this peaceful oasis, with oats, water, shade and plenty of grass, away from the vast, arid expanse of undulating, stubbled and ploughed land. "The first place of man and the first place for grass" was how Santiago described it. We were all exhausted after walking for 12 days. I had blisters on my feet and my back ached from lifting the heavy grain onto the saddle so many times. The only way I could get up was to roll on to my side and lever myself up with my hands.

A reporter who came to interview me in Spanish, told me that what I was doing was dangerous and advised me to keep the police informed of my whereabouts at all times. Although I was so tired, I didn't allow fear to enter my mind, as God had taken care of us so far and directed us to this resting place, and I was confident that he would continue to look after us. When the reporter left, I lay back on the grass and for the first time ever, I also saw Ermis lie down to sleep.

I hoped David wouldn't mind that we didn't catch him up, as I'd decided to rest another day in our oasis. It was good to step aside, as I'd almost felt myself swept along with some of the other pilgrims and their competitive race to cover the distance. Many had to drop out as they had pushed themselves too hard. It was not a race to Santiago, but a time to contemplate, although I knew it was best to reach our destination before the snow arrived.

Success is a journey, not a destination. - Robert Schuller

We left our special place in Atapuerca while it was still dark, the ponies' hooves echoing on the paved streets. By the time we reached the outskirts of the village it was pouring with cold rain, so we increased our pace to warm up and get to our destination before it turned to snow. As we followed the rocky track up the hill, past stubbled fields, I was even more thankful to have found our oasis, as there wasn't a blade of grass to be seen. Above 1,000 metres it was even more windswept, with no trees to provide shelter. I lost sight of the Camino signs, but from the top of the escarpment I could see the city of Burgos in the distance – I needed to pass through it and find a safe place to camp on the other side.

The combine harvesters were busy, as were huntsmen shooting birds. I'd been surprised by the lack of wildlife in the great expanses of northern Spain, but after seeing men with guns shooting even the little birds, I concluded that there were few of them left. As I neared the outskirts of the city, I saw three deer bounding through the harvested crops and I willed them to stay away from the countryside, and to remain in the relative safety of the city outskirts.

54. Burgos

 Somehow I got back onto the Camino track, just when I wanted to avoid it, because it followed ten kilometres of main road into Burgos – a city of almost 200,000 people. There was one advantage however: at least we could stop and graze in the city's irrigated green spaces, and as it was Sunday and siesta time, no one told me to move! We walked on through smelly, polluted streets and jostled with cars, whose drivers were often impatient to get to their Sunday afternoon destination. I was just glad it wasn't a work day, as it would have been even more frenetic.

Once we got into the old city, the pavements were so narrow that we had to walk in the middle of the road, sometimes down one-way streets in the wrong direction, against the flow of traffic. I was constantly on the lookout, making sure that Yoana and Ermis didn't scrape or scratch any vehicles. I was also hoping they wouldn't poop, but Ermis did, so I use the water bucket to scoop it into a bin (after that they refused to drink from the bucket, even when I'd washed it out). I had no food, so I found a grassy spot, tethered them and ran into a shop – one of the very few to be open on a Sunday – and grabbed some bread and cheese (which later turned out to be butter!). When I got back, the ponies were surrounded by a crowd of excited people, and children who were asking to touch them. Everyone was enjoying the ponies, except one disgruntled woman who grumbled away at a man who allowed his children to stroke Ermis. He just ignored her, and was an example to me: you will always get spoilsports – just shrug it off!

I followed the Camino through the narrow streets of Burgos, which is known as the Gothic capital of Spain and was once the seat of Franco's government. Suddenly, Burgos Cathedral, one of the biggest and grandest in Spain, appeared before me in all its magnificence. I felt as if I'd walked onto a film set.

"Hi Tracey, can I get you a drink?" said an American voice. "It's David – remember, we met about ten days ago?" I was happy to receive such a friendly greeting from David, a pilgrim from North America, who introduced me to his friend Cibele, from Brazil, and I asked if he could take some photos of us in front of the cathedral.

"Can you try and get the top of the cathedral in?" I asked, when checking the picture on the back of my camera. "I'll try!" he replied, and we laughed as he made four attempts to fit it all in. He got there in the end, and I was grateful for his perseverance. David then kindly held my ponies as I took a quick look inside the cathedral, where the famous El Cid, his horse Babieca and his wife were all buried.

"El Cid, also known as Count Rodrigo Diaz de Vivar, a legendary son of Burgos, was born in 1043," I read. El Cid became the chief general to Alfonso VI, and led his fight against the Moors, but was later exiled and went on to command a Moorish force himself. El Cid was recalled to service by Alfonso, and created his own fiefdom in the city of Valencia, where he died in 1099. El Cid's body, along with that of his wife and horse, was eventually brought back to Burgos Cathedral.

I then rushed to the tourist information centre to ask about accommodation for the ponies, only to find it was siesta until four. So I thanked David and hurried to get out of the city and find a sheltered camp, as a wild and dark sky threatened to turn into a big storm.

Hontanas

The St. Anthony's archway where bread used to be left for pilgrims. An old 11th century monastery founded by the Antonine Order in France and connected to the work of Saint Anthony of Egypt, patron saint of animals. Here I met a 70 old woman from Toulouse carrying her own back pack.

55. Muddy Meseta

A cyclist from Paris stopped for a chat while my ponies were grazing on alfalfa. He'd been unable to buy food as it was Sunday, and was hungry, so I gave him half my bread and half my pack of butter and he went on his way. Yoana who was also hungry, bit a hole in the grain sack and it poured onto the ground. I never liked waste, especially valuable grain, and would usually have waited for them to eat it all up, but it was getting dark and I wanted to find shelter before the storm broke.

As I followed a track a rabbit, the first I had seen, darted out in front of us. Further along, I found a hedge, a screen of bamboo and a grassy verge, so I pitched my tent here. I had trouble getting the tent pegs into the hard ground but I persisted, as I could see a big storm approaching. The wind blew ferociously all night and, in the early hours it felt as if the sky had exploded. The following morning, I searched for the big yellow mac which Paolo had given me in Italy, but could only find a flimsy red one. I retraced our steps and was relieved to find it lying on the road. The rain was still lashing down and the ponies didn't want to go forwards – they just swivelled their hindquarters into the prevailing wind.

We crossed over the northern edge of the Meseta plateau (950m), where eagles soared and an army of windmills strode across the horizon, and the rain hit us horizontally. My fingers were so cold, and my boots and the ponies' hooves were caked in mud, making every step laborious, although we did pass some people on bicycles. They had overtaken us earlier, but were now stuck in the mud.

Every time a bicycle approached from the rear and surprised them, the ponies would shoot forwards. On one occasion, Yoana ripped my prized saddle bags off Ermis. On another, they surged ahead so fast that I had to dive to one side to avoid being trampled, banging my knee on a stone wall and ripping my waterproof trousers – the third time this same knee had been whacked on my European journey. The ponies quickly stopped and looked back at me, wondering why was I was lying on the ground clutching my leg. I was just relieved that they hadn't taken off at a gallop, as my American horses used to do, and crashed into café tables in the village a little way ahead.

At this café I met a man who told me to find Paco, another man in the next town called Castrojeriz, who had accommodation for the ponies. I continued on my way hoping I would be able to find this man Paco and that he could also help me to find grain.

Castrojeriz was a major stopping point on the medieval Camino, with eight pilgrim hospitals sitting beneath a 9th century hilltop castle. I arrived at the albergue to find that it was shut, so asked in a neighbouring shop if they knew where I could find Paco. The man pointed, but I got lost and ended up on the far side of town, where most of the houses' roofs were falling in and their walls were crumbling, as the dry earth bricks lacked durability. I spotted a farmyard, containing big harvesting machinery, and asked if they had oats for sale. They didn't, but at least they knew Paco, and directed me back into town.

At last I found the right door, knocked, and there was Paco. He showed me to some smart, new stables on the outskirts of town – so new that they were unprepared for horses and had no hard grain or hay. Paco was most helpful, and took me in search of oats. None of the feed merchants on the outskirts of the town had any, so we drove on across the plains.

"This is the first rain for four months," he told me, chatting away in Spanish. I caught the gist of what he was saying, but a lot of it went right over my head. At one point he was telling me about his dog, who had his head out the car window and knocked over a road sign.

Castrojeriz, a place rich in history, with Roman and Visigothic remains, ruined monasteries and a ninth century castle on the hilltop.

I said a quick prayer as I could smell beer on Paco's breath – we'd got this far, thanks to God's protection, and I certainly wanted to avoid a road accident. After driving for about 10 kilometres, we found a helpful grain merchant and I bought 30 kilos – a mixture of oats and barley – at a very reasonable price.

Although the beautiful albergue was closed for the season, and some other pilgrims were turned away, Paco let me stay there all on my own, which I really appreciated. It was pouring with rain the following morning, and I'd left my coat with the ponies, so I used a black binliner for protection as I crossed the town to the stables.

The heavy oats soon became lighter, as I fed each pony five kilos a day. There was little grazing, and every three days, I'd be on the lookout for more. Ermis and Yoana would whinny to me at breakfast, lunch and tea, so when I ran out I felt really bad.

I was now wearing six layers of clothing, plus a woolly hat and gloves, but we warmed up as we climbed over the high plains and crossed from Burgos to the Palencia region. Tractors towing harrows frantically crossed to and fro, racing until dark to prepare the soil before the winter rains. That night, I found a sheltered, hidden camping spot in a large gully and I prayed it wouldn't rain hard that night, in case we got washed away.

The Camino was very well signposted and pilgrims added some signs of their own.

Travelling through autumn colours.

 I was interested to see the Santa Maria la Blanca XIII in Villalcázar de Sirga as my guide book said it was worth a visit, telling Saint James' story and how he ended up in Galicia. I was surprised to find such a grand church in a relatively small town.

The autumn had been unusually warm, but the weather was now turning more wintery. I decided to feed the ponies high energy grain to quicken our pace, so that we'd no longer be the slowest on the Camino. At one point, the signs directed us across the road and into the town of Carrión de los Condes.

I'd become conscious of a figure walking on the other side of the road, keeping pace with us. "De dónde? Norway?" I asked him, recognising a Norwegian flag on a cup hanging from his backpack, but he said he was from San Sebastián in the Basque region. He suggested a coffee, so I tethered the ponies on a patch of good grass outside a café, much to their delight. The most nutritious grass at this time of year was usually found on irrigated lawns in the towns. Usually we were moved on, but not on this occasion.

He introduced himself as Ricardo, and I soon found out that his English was more fluent than my Spanish, so we spoke a bit of both languages. He had recently taken early retirement from a life-long job with Michelin and was walking to find out what God would have him do next. When we'd finished our coffee, he carried on walking while I went to buy some credits for my phone. The shop assistant was having difficulty understanding me, but then Ricardo reappeared and helped me out.

Once again he marched off in front, but we were reunited on the edge of town and walked together across the harvested wheat plains, with small eagles soaring overhead. I realised that I'd only seen one rabbit on my journey through Spain and wondered if they'd all been eaten, shot or had just got wise to the dangers of venturing out in daylight.

Reunited with David who played his didgeridoo at a picnic spot.
Below: Ricardo leading Yoana.
Below left: Yoana and Ermis saying hello to the pilgrim statue.

56. Roman Road

Knowing that the testing of your faith produces endurance. James 1v3 NKJ

'Don't stop me now!' was etched on a stop sign by the road, and made me chuckle. I knew exactly what they meant, although walking with Ricardo did mean I had to keep pace with his famous "six kilometres an hour".

'He died so that YOU can live' was scratched on another sign and I understood this one too: Jesus died for our sins, in place of us, that whosoever believes in Him would not die (spiritually) but have eternal life.

Another one read: 'It's not about church, it's about Him'. On the way to Santiago there are so many grand, beautiful and historic monuments built in God's honour. For me, it's not just in the buildings that I find God – it's about a living, breathing relationship with Jesus in my heart. As Paul the Apostle said: "God who made the world and everything in it, since he is Lord of heaven and earth, does not dwell in temples made with hands... so we should seek the Lord, in hope that we might find Him, though He is not far from each one of us; for in Him we live and move and have our being."

'I just want to go home' was scribbled on another sign, which made me smile too. That's how I'd felt a few days earlier, when I was exhausted, cold and had little food for my hungry ponies. This walk was certainly a test of endurance – no wonder there were so many hospitals on the Camino. I had a nasty cough, and was all too aware of this when I slept in the 'albergues' (hostels). I knew it kept people awake, even when I coughed into my sleeping bag – sometimes I felt as if I was going to burst as I tried to restrain it. Ricardo was not much better off: he had been badly bitten by bedbugs.

The weather was cold that night so I went to an albergue with Ricardo, even though there was little grass for the ponies. The next day was warmer, but dark rain clouds were approaching across the plains, so we kept going, hoping to outwalk them. It felt as if I was dragging the ponies to Santiago that afternoon, but Ricardo kindly took turns leading Yoana. We were following an old Roman road

when the storm clouds burst over us, but we pressed on, past several closed albergues. Finally, in the dark, after walking for 45 kilometres, we spotted one that was open in the back streets of Reliegos. I was grateful that the kind attendant gave me a large room to myself, where I could cough without disturbing anyone else. I fed and watered the ponies, hobbling on my swollen, blistered feet, and finally collapsed, exhausted, into my sleeping bag.

If you want the rainbow, you've gotta put up with the rain.
- Dolly Parton

Leaving our albergue at Reliegos

Yoana agrees it smells delicous: a grain mix at Mansilla de las Mulas.
Crossing one of the overhead metal bridges entering the city of León.

The only limitations are the ones you acknowledge.
- Buddy Harrison

"Tracey!" someone called, and I recognised the Koreans I'd met on my first day in Spain.

"I thought you'd be in Santiago by now," I exclaimed.

"We had foot problems," one of them explained, which was pretty usual for pilgrims.

Ricardo and I stopped in Mansilla de las Mulas – he always liked to have a coffee break in the morning and another in the afternoon.

"You are getting me into a coffee habit!" I told him. I'd always been a tea drinker, but it didn't taste good here. I enjoyed walking with Ricardo – he was learning English, and I was practising my Spanish. The ponies and I did struggle to keep up with his "six kilometres an hour", but when we fell behind, he would wait for us. We always tried to find grassy spots for our coffee breaks and were usually successful, although on the outskirts of cities they were spoilt by litter and once by a dead cat.

Ricardo helped me find more grain, even if it meant diverting off the Camino. In Mansilla de las Mullas we found sweetmeal mixed with molasses, which the ponies loved. However, they were both very, very familiar with where their delicious food was stored, and would try to bite holes in the sack. Yoana seemed to have a neck that was as pliable as a giraffe's, and could reach around and have a bite, so we had to use extra sacking to protect it.

I'd pulled a muscle across the ball of my foot during the previous day, adding to the pain from my usual blisters. I rode Ermis at times, but he was so slow that I could walk faster and lead them with less effort. It did sometimes feel as if I was dragging them to Santiago, and I asked myself how I could have two ponies and still end up walking all the way through Spain.

"She's got the grain!" said a passing Australian, pointing to Yoana. Ricardo and I were on a bridge, discussing a possible photo, and looked round to see that she'd bitten through the sack and grain was pouring onto the ground. We quickly managed to patch the holes up with plastic bags, making sure that if any more precious food escaped, it would not be wasted on the ground.

Ricardo walked on the outside to protect the ponies from the traffic as we entered the big city of León. We were directed to the city racecourse, amid betting stalls and stables. There was no one around, so I picked the grassiest spot, tethered the ponies to separate trees and left a note saying we'd be back after booking ourselves into the albergue. I hobbled on through the cold night, still wearing my walking boots, as my sandals had broken some time ago.

León is a smart, cosmopolitan city – its name derived from 'legion', reflecting its origins as a Roman military garrison. It was once the capital of the region, and was conquered and re-conquered by the Visigoths (Germanic people who defeated the Romans, sacked Rome in 410 AD and eventually settled in Spain and Portugal), and later by the Moors and Christian forces.

They never charged me for the ponies' accommodation, and although I appreciated the shower and being able to wash my clothes at the albergue, I'd have preferred to stay with them that night. I slept badly in that stuffy dormitory, blasted by a heater. I opened the window three times, as I could hardly bear it and couldn't suppress my coughing. I once left the dormitory to cough outside, and when I returned the window was closed.

"Ricardo, your next career could be with horses!" I joked, as he helped me load the grain, pack up Yoana in the dark and then shielded the ponies from the traffic as we left the city before the early morning rush hour.

57. Puente de Órbigo

Ricardo and an Italian pilgrim on Puente de Órbigo.

Puente de Órbigo is a beautiful 13th century bridge, built over an earlier Roman structure, with many arches leading to the Hospital de Órbigo. The bridge was also known as the passage of honour following a famous jousting tournament which took place in 1434. A noble knight called Don Suero de Quiñones, scorned by a beautiful lady, threw down the gauntlet to anyone who dared to pass over the bridge. Knights from all over Europe came to fight him, and only after he broke 300 lances did he continue on to Santiago, to offer thanks for his freedom from love and his restored honour.

After crossing the bridge, Ricardo and I parted company, as he booked into an albergue where there was no grass, so I couldn't stay there. We both felt a bit sad. Even though we'd only been walking four days together, we enjoyed each other's company and hoped we would meet again.

Although a little lost in thought, I enjoyed walking through the soft, warm evening light, and was joined for a while by an Italian pilgrim who I'd met earlier. My ability to speak Italian had deserted me, so I tried Spanish, which he seemed to understand a little. He stopped at the next village, but the land was still barren so I continued up a stony track into an open expanse of tussock grassland. Here, I found a place to camp, under some trees with long, dry grass for the ponies.

Camping on my own, I felt relaxed, not trying to suppress coughs, and was up early before the shooting began, as it always seemed to on Sundays.

I made sure my yellow mac was very visible. as I travelled through the expanse with straw bales and windmills highlighted by the early sun.

58. Astorga

On the outskirts of Astorga, we took a grass break beside a field of sweetcorn, but the ponies soon discovered it to be tasty, so I had to move them away. I hoped Ricardo would march this way from the Hospital de Órbigo, as this was much the prettier route, even if it was a bit longer. I estimated the time he would arrive, at his usual 6 kilometres an hour and, sure enough, I soon saw his familiar silhouette in the distance, so we continued together into Astorga. This city has been an important road junction ever since Roman times, as the meeting point for several pilgrim routes and the royal drove roads – a European-wide system of nomadic grazing, when animals were herded up and down the Iberian peninsula. This is still celebrated today, when sheep are driven through the town.

Sheep may have been popular here, but not my ponies. The police came after us when I failed to notice that one of my ponies had left droppings in the road. By the time I got back there, it had been plastered to the tarmac by passing cars. I could never understand how people could get so upset over a bit of horse manure – it was only harmless, digested grass.

To avoid more pony poo issues, we didn't linger long in the city, but continued onto Murias de Rechivaldo. Here, Ricardo found a restaurant where we could enjoy the famous, traditional Maragato cuisine, which consisted of a substantial amount of meat (tender, with fat), accompanied by cabbage and chick peas, followed by soup and then by flan, and all at a very reasonable price. Usually I can eat everything, but this was the only meal in Europe which I couldn't finish!

I enjoyed travelling with Ricardo because he introduced me to all sorts of local specialities along the Camino. He was from Spain, although he would reminded me proudly: "I am not Spanish – I am Basque!"

We climbed up to La Cruz de Ferro, an iron cross standing 1,505 metres above sea level – the highest point on the Spanish stretch of the Camino. The descent was very rough and steep, so whenever we had the option, we followed the winding road. It began raining and was getting cold and dark as we passed two closed albergues, and eventually found an open one on the far side of Molinaseca. As winter approached, we would pass more and more closed albergues. The Camino was much quieter now, in contrast to August when over 27,000 pilgrims followed this route – I'd even heard of pilgrims setting off at 3am to guarantee a bed at the next town. I had also noticed many new albergues being built – clearly the Camino was bringing prosperity to towns and villages along the way – but I was very glad I wasn't travelling during a busy month, even if the weather was a bit rough at times.

I tethered the ponies in the sparse garden, but they had a good grain feed. Even though we'd completed 30 mountainous kilometres that day, we both summoned up the energy to complete yet another kilometre back to town, through the rain, to buy supplies and supper.

Ricardo picking edible cactus fruit.
(below) Showers move across the hillside with us.

59. Ponferrada

One of the best preserved Templar castles in Spain is to be found at Ponferrada. When the Crusaders lost the Holy Land, many religious and chivalrous orders were created, all dedicated to protecting the pilgrim route through Spain to Santiago and St. James' grave. The Knights Templar are the source of many mysteries, and their rising influence became a threat to the Papacy and Catholic Monarchies. On Friday 13th 1307, the Pope and King Philip of France joined forces, captured the Grand Master of the Templar Order, and put him to death. Friday the 13th has been considered unlucky ever since!

As we approached this sturdy castle, I was so surprised when Ricardo swung open a gate in the moat wall to allow the ponies to graze in the clover and long grass. Meanwhile, we drank coffee in a café opposite and found a grain store. We left Ponferrada by the bridge which gave the city its name, as it was reinforced with iron as far back as the 11th century. Both coal and iron have been mined in the area ever since.

The 12th century Templar castle and (above) Ricardo with the ponies besides a pilgrim mural.

We are all travellers in the wilderness of this world and the best we can find in our travels is an honest friend.

- Robert Louis Stevenson

The area has a unique micro climate, ideal for the Bierzo wines, and we passed extensive vineyards along the way. By now, all three of Ermis' saddle attachments around the cantel (back of the saddle) had been pulled off by Yoana – the first one at the very beginning of my journey, in Greece, and the other two in Spain. It meant I had nowhere to hang my coats, or to attach Yoana, as I occasionally led her with a piece of string tied to the saddle. The only exception was when we were passing tempting alfalfa grass (which they could always spot at a distance). She would literally pull both me and Ermis off the track to get a bite to eat. I was sure these were her survival tactics, learnt in Greece. I would really like to have known more about the history of my ponies, but the Greek horse dealer had not been forthcoming. Yoana would eat anything, and I guessed she had suffered malnutrition the previous year, judging by the grooves in her hoof walls. To prevent her yanking us off the track, I had to lead her off the bit, but the lack of attachments was a problem.

"You know, I was the best mechanic before I retired," stated Ricardo, as he fixed the attachments back onto the saddle, using some nails that he'd just bought. He added, with a smile: "But now I am an adventurer!"

60. Galicia

Every life comes with a story …. And a possibility for a great adventure.
– Kobi Yamada

The landscape changed abruptly as we left the pastel hues of autumn and the open vineyard regions of Castilla and León behind us. We climbed into the damp landscape of Galicia, dotted with livestock, enclosed by hedges in small fields. In the rain, we met a pilgrim called Patrick who had walked all the way from Amsterdam with his bull dog. He said this had caused problems – people were especially wary of offering accommodation to someone with this breed of dog – so he'd had to camp all the way, which was much more uncomfortable now it was wet and cold. I was surprised to see that Galicia was so green and grassy after our long walk through dry parched plains, but I soon experienced the westerly Atlantic weather which hit this north western province of Spain, depositing lashings of cold rain.

It was almost is if we'd entered another country – so far removed from the arid, arable plains of northern Spain. On we went, almost dragging Yoana and Ermis, who enjoyed the plentiful grass but didn't like the weather. Ermis, in particular, disliked the driving rain getting into his ears so he laid them back, lowered his head and walked right beside me, trying to shelter from the wind.

It was dark and the rain was still pouring down when we found an open albergue. The owner kindly offered her garage to the ponies, but it had a concrete floor with no bedding and no hay, so I had to tether them outside, under a big tree and beside a hedge, offering slight shelter from the deluge.

Galicia reminded me of the west of Ireland, with its landscape of small fields, shrouded in mist and rain, but also because of the lack of employment for its large families, many of whom had left to find work.

The trail led us through the ancient, cobbled streets of O'cebreiro, which had accommodated pilgrims for hundreds of years, and past its 9th century church – one of the oldest surviving buildings on the Camino de Santiago.

"We've got to get out of these hills!" I remarked when we stopped to shelter and eat lunch, and heard that snow was forecast for the following day. As we approached the albergue, we walked through lush grass and the ponies plunged their heads down to eat, unused to finding such ample food at their feet.

"Esto es Galicia (this is Galicia)," exclaimed the friendly caretaker. "We have much rain and grass. You can leave a horse here – no hay problema (no problem)."

Ricardo and the ponies at the Alto do San Roque across from the Monumento do Peregrino in the wind and rain. Below: O'cebreiro with its distinctive stone buildings which made up part of the 11th century monastic settlement.

And in the sweetness of friendship let there be laughter,
and sharing of pleasures.
For in the dew of little things the heart finds its morning and is refreshed.
- Kahlil Gibran

Ricardo took turns leading the ponies along the tracks, through autumn-coloured beech woods and between fields of dairy cows. Suddenly I felt a tendon or muscle ping across the ball of my foot, and it hurt to walk – far worse than the constant blisters on my toes – so Ricardo told me to ride, but I'd almost got out of the habit. Ermis had at one stage been carrying the grain, but it kept shifting, so Yoana ended up carrying the extra weight. In fact, Ermis had been getting off lightly, as I'd led him most of the way through northern Spain – I wanted to give him a break as he'd lost weight. He was so stubborn: when he followed, attached by a 'pigging string' to Yoana's pack, he kept snapping it, but when I tried leading him, I'd virtually have to drag him along. I wasn't sure whether it used up more energy leading him or riding him, but I needed to rest my foot. Knowing that many pilgrims before me had abandoned their pilgrimage because they pushed themselves too hard, I decided to ride him.

The weather was rough that night so we had to press on to find an open albergue with grass. We all needed a rest, but I didn't want to miss the horse transporter which was due to pick up the ponies in Santiago and transport them back to England the following week. I was concerned that Ermis didn't eat his grain, and wondered if it was because of the roasted chestnuts that we'd shared.

The next day, we had our usual picnic of cheese and bread, as the ponies grazed. We felt sad, despite the colder, wetter weather, as the Camino markers showed that Santiago was now getting close, especially at Ricardo's six kilometres an hour – although he'd often have to wait for us, twirling his stick.

"Always media media (half and half)," stated Ricardo as we shared our food, and added: "I tell you, we made half the Camino together."

"But when I met you, you were the fastest person on the trail!" I laughed. "We slowed you down!"

"Yes, six kilometres an hour," he chuckled. "But now I like to go with you, Ermis and Yoana. I have never talked with horses before!" We'd become good walking companions, and Ricardo would help me find grain, which often meant diverting several kilometres off our route.

"We make our own Camino!" exclaimed Ricardo as we headed off the trail again to replenish our grain supply. Often, we could only find 40kg sacks, so we'd give them a good feed on the spot and then split the remainder and load it onto Yoana's pack. I knew she felt the extra weight, but she was an amazingly tough mare. As the ponies ate their way through it, the pack got 10kg lighter each day, and by the fifth day, it was all gone, so we had to find another grain store.

Ricardo and the ponies passsing a Horreos, a stone granary particular to Galicia, where the harvest, mostly maize, is stowed out of reach from rats and rain.

Ricardo leading the ponies up the street of Melide

61. Poison in Melide

That night, we arrived at a small albergue in the village of Eirexe, and once again, it was already dark. My heart sank when I was told to put the ponies in a barren park, but a Romanian girl (who lived in Spain) found us a large grassy garden.

"Stay away from the vegetable garden," she said seriously. I was so grateful, and took care to tether them well away from the vegetables, as I knew they would eat anything. While the ponies contentedly grazed, we had a meal at the village café. The TV was on full blast – as was usual in the restaurants, bars and coffee shops of northern Spain. I always tried to sit facing away from the screen, otherwise I'd become transfixed like everyone else. Most of the locals in cafés seemed to be men, and Ricardo confirmed that this was the norm in rural Spain.

Our next stop was Melide, where we stopped for a late afternoon coffee.

"The police wanted to issue a ticket to your horses for being on the grass," said Ricardo, who was speaking to an old man on a bicycle. "But this man asked them not to." The kind man then led us to what he described as "a very grassy spot", but in reality it was overgrown with weeds and brambles. Ermis didn't eat anything, but as usual Yoana managed to find some grazing.

The albergue was a large modern building with four dormitories, but with 30 people squashed into each. The sour receptionist wouldn't allow me to bring my saddles and packs indoors, so two ladies helped Ricardo and me to move them to the back – I just had to hope they wouldn't be stolen. After dining on octopus (a local speciality) we returned to the albergue to find that we'd been locked out. Even though I'd slimmed down during my travels, I still couldn't squeeze in through a partially open window. Eventually someone heard us and opened the door, but I wasn't at all comfortable at the thought of being crammed into a dormitory, like a sardine in a tin, with the heaters blasting, keeping everyone awake with coughing. I was also concerned about leaving the ponies alone in a city surrounded by derelict buildings, so I grabbed my sleeping bag and pitched my tent next to them.

I awoke to hear one of the ponies stumbling around and groaning. I scrambled to put my boots on, grabbed a torch and found Yoana staggering, her hind legs not holding her up. I comforted her and prayed, wondering if she'd eaten something poisonous, as Ermis was unperturbed and was sleeping on his feet. I let them both loose and kept watching her, but got so cold that I had to get back into my sleeping bag to warm up. Then I got worried when I couldn't hear anything, so I checked the ponies again only to see Yoana flat out on the ground.

"Oh God, don't let her be dead, please don't let her be dead!" I pleaded, as I approached her still body.

I reached out my hand to touch her still head and immediately she burst into life, her head jerked up and she bared her teeth at the shock of being awakened.

"Oh God, thank You!" I gasped as she got up, seemingly much better. In the morning, I awoke to find Ermis nuzzling the tent. "Don't bite a hole in the roof!" I scolded him, remembering how they'd bitten through the grain sack. I scrambled up to give them both breakfast, so thankful for Yoana's miraculous recovery, and Ricardo then helped to lift the panniers onto Yoana.

I was glad to leave the heaviness of Melide and get back into the country. We stopped for our usual picnic in lovely grassy parkland, where we met Roberto, another pilgrim, asleep on a wall. We shared our picnic with him, and he gave us pâté and peppers. The place was so peaceful and grassy that I wanted to stay the night there, but it was too early. Elena, the Romanian girl who we'd met in Eirexe, caught up with us and we were also joined by a Belgian man. Ricardo strode off at his usual speed, but waited for us, swinging his famous walking stick, which he had left behind at numerous cafés.

That night, I was happy to stay in a country albergue, with a field for the ponies, and only eight people in the dormitory. As with all the government albergues, it only cost €5 a night – half the price of the privately owned albergues, making the long walk through Spain more affordable. The next day, on the outskirts of Santiago, we passed a riding stables where the price per pony was a staggering €40 a night. However, with Ricardo as interpreter, they were very helpful and agreed to take us to the Ministry vet in order to check their papers for the journey back to England.

"It is not possible to travel with these documents here," stated the vet, waving my ponies' passports for which I had paid a lot of money. "You should have had another certificate to leave Italy."

"But I went to the Ministry vet in Italy, and waited a whole week for the correct documents, blood tests and everything!"

"These papers are no good for travelling in these countries – you need another certificate," he repeated, but no one seemed to know exactly what certificate I actually needed.

"Our plans have changed," said the English horse transporter. "You'll have to pay double now because we'll have to make a detour from Madrid to pick your two up. Let me know."

"I can let you know now. No!" I replied, as this would mean paying almost £4,000 to get my ponies home to England, and to make matters worse, they wouldn't take me with the ponies because they said they didn't have insurance. "Incredible," I thought. "I've just travelled across Europe, with ponies, and without insurance. Now we can't even get a lift home together." Later I heard that they transported horses worth over £140,000, so no wonder they could ask whatever price they liked.

With Ricardo's help, a local Spanish transporter came to the stables. "Your ponies are only worth €600 for the pair of them," he laughed. "They are not worth transporting."

"Affection costs," commented Ricardo.

"Well, so what if they are not worth much? Some things, like loyalty, are worth much more – especially after all we have been through together." I resolved to get them home, even if it meant walking to France and crossing the Channel. I refused to leave them in Spain.

Another man said he would transport them to Lyon, in France, for €2,000 depending on what cattle he was carrying. I didn't want them being squashed in with cows, which might have horns, and I didn't want to be dropped in the middle of France either – especially at that price.

We passed several memorials to people who had died on the Camino. Sometimes their shoes would be there, maybe a photo of people from all over the world. At some spots there would be piles of stones, rather like those I had seen in Tibet, or bits of clothing, or stick crosses or messages.

(below) A fellow pilgrim feeding grapes to Ermis and (above right) studying the map.

62. Santiago de Compostela

On November 9th, after walking over 790km through northern Spain, we arrived triumphantly at Santiago de Compostela and the Praza Obradoiro square. Here we were reunited with some familiar Camino pilgrims, others from Alaska, South Africa and Belgium… and the inevitable Spanish policeman.

"I've met more policemen in Spain than vets in Europe!" I exclaimed while Ricardo was arguing – insisting we had permission to enter the square.

"We have to leave now," he shrugged.

"Well, hey Ricardo, we made it to Santiago!" I added with a cheer. "And we got some pictures!"

But my exuberance was shattered the following morning. Ricardo had walked into our lives just two weeks previously, and now he was walking away. I felt sad to say goodbye, but grateful that our paths had crossed, as his good company had enriched my journey.

Now I had to seriously practise my Spanish, but fortunately I found help at the Hipica la Lagunita stables, in the form of the owner Requina and her sister Monica. So I left the ridiculously complicated Spanish paperwork with them and we headed for Finistere – 'the end of the world'. According to ancient legend, Saint James preached Christianity on the Iberian Peninsula and his disciples brought his body back here after his death. Hundreds of years later some bones were found and attributed to Saint James, and this discovery led to the founding of Santiago de Compostela.

As we passed through the city, I was reunited with David, who showed me the symbol of freemasonry, right at the heart of the cathedral's ornate ceiling. During my travels it had become obvious that the church was intertwined with an intricate tapestry of influences, combining Christendom, religious mysticism, paganism and so much more. No wonder Jesus came to set us free, saying: "I am the way and the truth and the life. No one comes to the Father except through Me" (John 14v6). In other words, he said, "it's all about a relationship with Me!"

I bade farewell to David, who was now walking back to France, and continued westwards. I half hoped and expected to see Ricardo waiting for us around the next corner, twirling his famous stick, but he wasn't there. I felt sad, but at the same time grateful, as our trio continued alone – that's how we had started, six months previously in Greece, and how we would end our journey in north west Spain.

Arriving in the Prazo Obradoiro in Santiago de Compostela where, innocent of pony poo, the police are after us as usual!

63. Finistere – Muxia Way

It was late in the day when I left Santiago, with only a few hours of daylight remaining to find a secure place to camp. We followed the Finistere-Muxia Way, used by some pilgrims to reach the Costa da Morte (Coast of Death), and eventually found some large gorse bushes – big enough to conceal my tent and ponies. Much rain fell that night and continued through the following day and night. It was still falling when I arrived at Olveiroa, and was shown to a dirty concrete cattle shed with no bedding, for which I'd have to pay €10 a pony! I said they'd be better off on the grass, in the rain. However, a generous local farmer, who was drinking at the albergue, offered us his barn and grass for free. I was grateful for this, especially when I found that the ponies had the choice of sheltering in the open barn, with its straw-covered earthen floor, or grazing in the rain, and were securely locked in by the farmer. So securely, that I couldn't get them out the following morning – I think he wanted us to stay forever! I was helped by Thorsten, a very tall German and an experienced pilgrim who had walked several of Spain's Camino trails. We lifted the packs over the locked gate, so that I could pack up the ponies to leave, while Thorsten went in search of the farmer and the key.

Thorsten and the local farmer with the ponies at Olveiroa passing several stone granaries which are particular to Galicia for storing crops. (Left) Rua das Hortas, Santiago de Compostela.

It had barely stopped raining since we had crossed the regional border into Galicia – such a contrast to the high plains, which we had passed through just weeks ago, where it hadn't rained for four months. I continued to follow the concha shell signs towards Finistere, but had been warned by the tourist information centre in Santiago that I needed to remember every turn, as there were no signs facing in the opposite direction (I guess most people without ponies took the bus back!). At every junction I would look back at the way I had come, and take a mental picture. We were passing through a maze of wooded tracks and small villages, and I didn't want to get lost on the return journey.

The nearer we got to the sea, the stronger the wind blew, and I had to hold onto my hat. When I found a more sheltered place to feed grain to the ponies, the wind dried my tent in 20 minutes. I stopped again in a town and I tied the ponies on some grass, before running into a shop to grab some supplies. The security guard was quick, and was waiting for me when I reached the checkout. "Peligrino, vamos ahora (I'm a pilgrim and I'm going now)," I said dashing out.

Everything was moving in the wind, signs were rattling and boats were bobbing on the waves. I was aiming for an albergue in Finistere, but when darkness fell, I suddenly felt exhausted and decided to make camp inland, amongst trees and reeds. The tent almost got blown away – I grabbed it and groped about for the tent pegs amongst the twigs, before quickly putting my bedroll and camera inside to weigh it down. As I was eating my bread and cheese in the darkness, car headlights briefly illuminated the ponies, so I quickly hid them back in the reeds and trees and gave them more grain.

The sea and wind roared loudly all night, accompanied by thunder and lightning, while torrential rain hammered on the tent and began to seep in. I was hoping we wouldn't be flooded out, as I'd pitched the tent on a slope near a ditch, and hadn't expected such a big storm. As I lay there, my feet throbbing, I had to dismiss thoughts of the sea crashing over the sand dunes – the only barrier between us and the beach.

Floods at Finistere and (right) crossing the Maceira Bridge.

The route took us through an alleyway which became narrower and narrower. When Yoana's packs were scraping along the walls, I held my breath, concerned that if it continued to narrow she could be wedged and we had come too far along the alley to reverse back out.

64. The End of the World!

After a sleepless night, I slipped damp socks over my blistered feet and scrambled out to survey the situation. It was still dark, but during flashes of lightning and I could see that the ditch had filled up and water was lapping at the edge of the tent. Ermis, who disliked getting his feet wet, was separated from us by another gulley of water, so I had to find a way around it to untie him and move to higher land where we could get packed up. We hadn't got far when we reached more rushing water – I didn't know how deep it was, so took a detour inland, before heading back towards the coast. We were continually blasted by sand, making it even harder to take photos, and as soon as I tried, all Ermis wanted to do was roll.

The strong wind blew me sideways on the final stretch to the lighthouse, and we had to lean into it to make progress. We arrived at the top to find the place deserted, apart from a tarpaulin, stretched across a corner for shelter, with a bicycle and a pair of boots beside it! I also found our last concha shell marker – that faithful sign which had counted down the kilometres to Santiago.

This place was called the 'End of the World' from a time when the earth was thought to be flat. As I struggled to make sure we weren't blown onto the rugged rocks and waves below, I could also see why it was called the Coast of Death. This was once the site of pagan rituals, and the Romans regarded it as the place where the sun vanished into the sea. Right up until the late Middle Ages, it was the last piece of explored land in Western Europe, and the final stage of a road that appeared to be mirrored in the sky by the Milky Way.

At first, we were the only ones braving the bad weather, but eventually others turned up and I asked them to take a few snapshots of us.

"It's time to go home ponies!" I told Ermis and Yoana, giving them each a pat, as we set off back to Santiago. Just before we left, I returned to the beach and picked up my own concha shell as my memorable souvenir.

Seek and you will find.
Do not be willing to accept an ordinary life.
– Salle Merrill Redfield

You could already know what you were designed to do, but maybe you don't and wonder – what is it all about anyway?
Do you ever have the nagging feeling there must be more to life?

It's in Christ that we find out who we are and what we are living for. Ephesians 1v12 TM

You can always ask Him: "Jesus, come into my life and show me what I was made for." And He'll show you and lead you through your own story – the good one He prepared in advance just for you!

In your book they were all written. The days fashioned for me. When as yet there were none of them, You saw me before I was born. Every day of my life was recorded in Your book. Every moment was laid out before a single day had passed. Psalm 139v16

227

Epilogue

It was tricky heading back to Santiago as I didn't have the help of concha shells to point the way and had to remember the landmarks – so much harder in the dark. I passed several people going in the other direction, but there weren't many pilgrims now on the Camino. I met Patrick, with his pet bulldog, who was heading to Finistere and then south to Portugal (he said it was too cold in Amsterdam in the winter) and I walked with Elias, a young Spanish man who had completed many of the Caminos in Spain – I enjoyed his company on the way back to Santiago.

As soon as we arrived in the square, we were welcomed by the policeman who threatened to fine me on the spot. So I didn't linger and crossed the city, back to the stables, where they kindly helped me to fill in the forms, exactly as required by the Ministry (it seemed that complex bureaucracy was to be found everywhere in Europe!). The Ministry vet wanted to help, and appreciated how difficult it was to know exactly what day and time the elusive transporter would pick up the ponies, where they would stop, and for how long – it took a lot of guesswork. But the papers only lasted for three days, and the transporter failed to show up within this time, so they had to re-do the papers all over again.

I finally got back to my home on Dartmoor, and Ermis and Yoana arrived a week later. As the driver unloaded them he told me he'd been travelling with racehorses worth over £100,000 and was surprised to see these two inconsequential little ponies coming all the way from Spain. However, I knew that these were incredible little ponies, who had come all the way from Greece and had proved their strength and loyalty time and again. I was excited to see them and Ermis was friskier that he'd ever been before, as they pranced through the village, their hooves echoing, eager to see their new home. At the Old Rectory, I let them loose and they immediately put their heads down to graze.

"There you go!" I reminded them. "When we were crossing Greece, Italy, Switzerland, France and Spain, I promised I would bring you home to the green grass of England!"

Four and a half months later, when Ermis and Yoana were on winter loan, I received a phonecall to tell me that Yoana had had a unexpected foal! We were all ecstatic, but it was short lived, as sadly he died ten days later of a suspected virus. It was incredible to think that Yoana had carried him all across Europe – what a tough little Greek horse! One day, when I have my own land (another dream!), I shall put her in foal again. Currently she is happily grazing with Callum, my Highland pony, who I rode from Scotland, while Ermis has been lent to a teenager, and they are having fun pony clubbing together. The latest news is that he's jumping well – what a contrast to his previous life in Greece! So these are two ponies with an incredible story to tell, even if we can only guess the first half!

Compostela means "field of dreams," and my hope is that our story has stirred you to dream and to live your own unique story. As the song goes, from South Pacific:

If you don't have a dream, how you gonna have a dream come true?

You are never too old to set another goal or dream a new dream. - C.S. Lewis

Going home!

ACKNOWLEDGEMENTS

Photos – with thanks to:

Remy Bois (Italian) 230 & Front Cover
Jonathan Constant (English) page 6
Annita Valvis (Greek) page 13
Diana Cawston (English) page 49, 51, 55, 57
Margaret Macdonald (English) page 52, 58, 59
Kalogiros Panagiotis (Greek) page 61
Elizabetha Gratia & Stephano (Italian) page 72
Paolo Vicario (Italian) page 78, 79, 80, 82, 91
Dimitri du Moulin (French) page 104,105,
Florence Chevallier (French) page 107
Anne Norris (Australian) page 108
Vuarambon François (French) page 111
Ali Gough (Scottish) top page 113
Jean Louis Kanzler (French) page 127, 128, 129
Gerda (German) page 140, 141, 142, 143
Tony Pobjie (Australian) Page 161, 162, 163
Denise Murphy (Irish) page 170
Norbert Szekeres (Hungary) page 178, 179
David Pomment (American) page 189 & back cover
Chantal Fauvel (Canadian) page 172
Ricardo Guarretxeria (Basque Spanish) page 198, 204, 206, 212, 213
Diana (English) page 218
Christina Whiting (Alaska) page 220, 221
Elias Oliver Albertos (Spanish) page 223, 224
Francine Stork (American) page 226, 228

www.en.wikipedia.org
A Pilgrim's guide to the Camino de Santiago by John Brierly